Teachable movie moments **from**
75 modern film classics

Videos
That
Teach

DOUG FIELDS
&
EDDIE JAMES

Youth Specialties

ZondervanPublishingHouse
Grand Rapids, Michigan
A Division of HarperCollinsPublishers

Videos That Teach: Teachable movie moments from 75 modern film classics

Copyright © 1999 by Doug Fields and Eddie James

Youth Specialties Books, 300 S. Pierce St., El Cajon, CA 92020, are published by Zondervan Publishing House, 5300 Patterson Ave. S.E., Grand Rapids, MI 49530.

Library of Congress-in-Publication Data

Fields, Doug, 1962-
    Videos that teach : teachable movie moments from 75 modern film classics / Doug Fields and Eddie James.
      p. cm.
    ISBN 0-310-23115-9
    1. Motion pictures in Christian education. 2. Christian education of teenagers.
I. James, Eddie. II. Title.
BV1535.4.F55   1999
268'.67—DC21   99-30113
                                           CIP

Edited by Sheri Stanley and Tim McLaughlin
Cover and interior design by DesignPoint, Inc.

Printed in the United States of America

99 00 01 02 03 04 05 06 / / 10 9 8 7 6 5 4 3

To Maria McNeill and David Smith, who turned
our ideas and scribbles into living words.

Acknowledgments

Many people have helped with this project in one way or another
reviewing the movie clips, trying out the ideas on their youth
groups, and encouraging us along the way.

Steve Chastain, Duane Cottrell, Kristy Davis, Ginny Lee Ellis,
Kathleen Hamer, Ronny Higgins, Bob Johns, Mike Katzenberger,
Linda Kaye, Mike Kinzer, Ted and Nancy Lowe, Ken Robertson, David
Rogers, Nicole Smith, Jeremy Webb, Angie and Tommy Woodard
thank you for being not only good youth workers, but good friends
as well.

Thanks also to the youth ministries at Saddleback Church and
First Woodway for allowing us to use videos while we teach.

And thanks to our incredible wives, Cathy Fields and Stephanie
James, who put up with late fees on movie rentals and flashlights
in theaters so we could take notes. We love you!

98219

Contents

Quick Clip Locator BY TOPIC

11

Quick Clip Locator BY BIBLE REFERENCE

So there I am, standing before a

group of students, teaching a lesson about God's grace that I just knew would be unforgettable (after all, it took several hours to prepare—besides, it was one of those messages that would make my preaching professor proud...if he were still alive).

Halfway through my lesson two guys in the back row start smacking each other. "Knock it off, jerk!" one of them says loudly.

Of course everyone turns around to see what's happening. I put on my Wounded Puppy Dog/Semi-Stern Pastor's Frown in a desperate attempt to communicate the hurt and disappointment I feel from watching these two punks effectively kill the learning experience for everyone in the room. At the same time four girls near the front put their heads together and whisper something to each other. A guy slouching in the middle of the room yells out, "Hey, Doug, when will this sermon be over?" Then a girl from the whispering quartet runs out of the room crying.

So much for the unforgettable lesson about grace. My mind shifts to law, and I imagine sacrificing a few students on the altar of my frustration. I vow never to teach students again.

Yet within 48 hours the memories of yet another hellfest begin fading. I repress the pain of failure and begin looking (again) for fresh ways to teach next week from God's Word. Although inevitably a journey of pain and privilege, it's a journey that can be made a little easier by the book you're now holding.

Esther, Everyman, and Ever After

The ancient Hebrews told patriarchal stories. Jesus told parables. The medieval church staged morality plays. And Hollywood has become our culture's premiere storyteller. Stories, whether read, recited, or enacted, have always gripped people's imaginations and emotions.

Movies are today's parables. Theater attendance is at a record high, multiplexes are being built everywhere, and the movie industry is making more money than ever before. Even if these facts make you wince, you can still see how *Videos That Teach* uses movies—that is, visual storytelling—to launch meaningful discussions that go beyond the surface of the script to kids' spirits, discussions that get kids talking about themselves and life and God.

Why use movie clips in youth meetings, anyway?

Many of your students are visual learners—which means they'll be impacted more by seeing a message than by merely hearing it. And whether we like it or not, that's how most students seem to be learning these days, living as we do in a culture saturated with visual media. An incessant, 24-hour stream of images on video, TV, movies, and the Internet surround us. Teenagers tend to be very comfortable with it all, and respond well to it.

Which is why video makes perfect sense if you want to grab your students' attention.

And clips from videotaped movies are among those visual tools. For years Doug used object lessons, "spontaneous melodramas," and a variety of other creative teaching methods to reinforce his Bible teaching. He always wanted to use video clips, but could never remember the right movie at the right time for the right message. His teaching changed when Eddie James joined him at Saddleback Church in Southern California. Eddie—whose mind is a virtual storehouse of movie and video clips—would do a quick mental search on the topic Doug was to speak on, and invariably come up with a clip to use. That gift of Eddie's quickly improved Doug's teaching and the students' interest.

FAQs

• *What about the copyright law?*

Motion pictures are fully protected by copyright. Public exhibition, especially when an admission fee is charged, could violate copyright. The copyright doctrine of fair use, however, permits certain uses of very brief excerpts from copyrighted materials for not-for-profit teaching purposes without permission. If you have specific questions about whether your plans to use film clips or other copyrighted materials in your lessons are permissible under these guidelines, you should consult your church's legal counsel. Or you or your church could apply for a blanket licensing agreement from the Motion Picture Licensing Corporation <www.mplc.com> for about $100 per year.

• *Why are some clips in this book from R-rated movies?**

Because none of the clips in *Videos That Teach*, even those from R-rated movies, contain language or content that is inappropriate or questionable to most youth groups.

Because clips from R movies (although the clips contain no R elements themselves) evoke very intense emotions and imagery—

---

*Here are the 11 movies: *Amistad, Braveheart, Dead Man Walking, The Ghost and the Darkness, Good Will Hunting, Jerry Maguire, Madonna: Truth or Dare, Malice, Planes, Trains, and Automobiles, A Time to Kill, When a Man Loves a Woman.*

Braveheart, A Time to Kill, and *Amistad,* for example.

Because sometimes, carefully, you can teach good theology by pointing to bad theology.

Because *of course* you'll preview *whatever* clip you want to use, to make sure it's appropriate for your lesson and for your group.

Because if, after you've previewed it, you're *still* unsure if it's suitable, you can always show it to your pastor, supervisor, or a parent for their opinion.

Because if you *still* don't feel comfortable using any of this book's 11 clips from R movies, there are still 64 clips here that are G, PG, or PG-13.

Because movie ratings are assigned by the dozen members or so of the ratings board of the Motion Picture Association of America <www.mpaa.org>—and the board's rating decisions are entirely subjective. Nor does the ratings board base its decisions on scriptural standards of conduct or of art. Ratings simply advise viewers about the level of "adult" content in a movie so parents can exercise appropriate control over what their underage children see.

You get the point. The use of a clip in this book does not imply endorsement of the movie in general, of other scenes in that movie in particular, of the actors' lifestyles, of the use of animals, firearms, or Scripture quotations in the movie, of the manufacturer of the cars used in the chase scenes—in short, we're not endorsing *anything.* This book simply lists 75 short clips, most of which (but not all of which) are appropriate and instructive to most youth groups (but not all youth groups) in most situations (but not all situations).

So you make the call. You're an adult. You're a leader of your youth group's teenagers. You know at what point instruction becomes distraction—for you, for your students, for their parents, for your church or organization. Use the summaries—and preview the clip before the lesson!—to discern which movie clips are too sophisticated for your middle schoolers, or too elementary for your senior highers. There's a lot to choose from here. Just think before you punch the play button.

- **Are you** sure *I need to preview a clip before showing it?*
If you don't preview a clip, you're asking for trouble—at the least it may cause you embarrassment, and at the most it may cost you your job. As you probably know, youth workers lose their jobs due to oversights like this. Protect yourself—preview the clip, and cue it up precisely.

Illustrating or building a lesson with Videos That Teach

Most youth workers use this book one of two ways:
- *You already have a lesson, and want a clip to illustrate it.*
Great—just flip to the "Quick Clip Locator—by topic" on page

9, find your topic, then turn to the corresponding clip. (If you're a browser, just leaf through the book with an eye on the upper right corners of the page spreads, where the topics of each clip are listed.) Or if your lesson is based on a Bible passage instead of a topic, check out the "Quick Clip Locator—by Bible reference" on page 15.

• *You simply want a change of pace in this week's youth meeting—and a movie-based lesson sounds good.* See the alphabetical list of movies in the table of contents for a movie you know and like, or just browse through the book until you find a clip that catches your interest.

What you'll find with each clip

Each of the 75 clips in *Videos That Teach* contains the same parts, clip to clip. Use as many or as few of the parts as you need to take your lesson where you want it to go. You can use just the clip to illustrate your own lesson...you can build a full-blown Bible study around the clip with the Scripture references provided (and with preliminary study on your part!)...you can trigger small-group discussions with any of several questions for each clip (with considerably less preparation). You know your students, so adapt or scavenge accordingly to meet their needs.

Here are the parts each clip includes:

Trailer

This is the leading question that gets kids' minds moving down the track of your topic (which are listed, by the way, in the upper-right corner of each clip's two-page spread). It gives you and your students an idea of what to watch and listen for as you view the clip.

For example, if you just jump into the clip of Happy Gilmore (Adam Sandler) punching a loud-mouthed spectator at a golf tournament (Bob Barker), all you'll get are students laughing at the outcome—without paying attention to the source of the conflict. On the other hand, if you set up your teaching time with a provocative question, students will still probably laugh at the clip—but underneath their laughter they'll get the point you're making. In fact, depending on how talkative a group you have, this opening question may trigger 15 or 20 minutes of discussion before you ever get to showing the clip.

The movie

If you're not familiar with a movie, this very brief summary helps you out. Even if you *do* know the movie, you can use (or read) the summary to explain the story line before you show a clip, if you want.

For a thorough, detailed description of the movie, get on

the Web, type "movie reviews" into your favorite search engine, and choose of the dozens of movie databases available. We found <www.empireonline.co.uk/reviews> particularly helpful. And <www.screenit.com> is "entertainment reviews for parents" of videos (and movies, music, and DVDs) that not only summarize the plot, but list in detail why the movie received the rating it did, with categories like violence, alcohol/drugs, guns/weapons, blood/gore, disrespectful/bad attitude, sex/nudity, imitative behavior, topics to talk about, etc.

This clip

With this detailed description of the clip itself, we've also listed the start and stop times of the clip. Simply rewind the video, set the counter to zero, and advance the movie to the time listed in the book. (Most VCRs have a real-time counter that lets you see the time of the movie as you're fast-forwarding it.) In case either the rental video or your VCR is different than ours, we've also included prompts from the movie—dialogue snippets or scene descriptions— to ensure that you start and stop it at the right time.

By the Book

The Bible is where you want your students to end up, sooner or later. If sooner, here's where you'll find Scriptures that are relevant to the clip's topic—to use for building a lesson from scratch, or as biblical input or direction for small-group discussions.

Where to take it

Here are several discussion questions, that generally try to bring together the clip's main point with the Bible passages listed earlier. Let the questions guide you, not coerce you. Tailor the questions to match the direction or depth of discussion your kids are capable of. This is the time to help them explore the meanings behind the clip, how the Bible speaks to that particular situation, and how it all applies to them.

Keep on teaching!

Trailer

Is the hope of Christ enough to get you through anything?

The movie drama, R

In 1839, La Amistad, a Spanish slave ship, set sail for the United States. The slaves on board rebelled against their captors. This movie follows the trial of Cinque (Djimon Hounsou), the slave who led the revolt.

This clip (just over 4 minutes)

 Start — 1:35:11

Prisoner makes a cross out of straw.

Stop — 1:39:12   *Judge prays in a church.*

An imprisoned slave is given a Bible containing pictures of the life of Christ, and by looking at them, he begins to see that Jesus changed everything. He pieces together the story of Christ, sharing what he understands with a fellow slave, and the two of them are able to find hope in a seemingly hopeless situation.

By the Book

Romans 12:12, 15:4; 1 Corinthians 15:19;
1 Thessalonians 5:8-10

Where to take it

📺 If you were one of the prisoners, would you have had hope after learning the message of Jesus?

📺 What more could the church have done for the slave than just give him a Bible? What can you do to help people understand more about Jesus and his message of salvation?

📺 Does the slave believe God will break the chains that bind him? Does he believe he will be cleared of all charges? What is the specific hope he has?

📺 What are some hopes you have? What are the hopes you can have when you know Christ?

📺 Have you ever completely given up hope? Were you able to find it again? How?

📺 How does hope help us get through difficult times?

📺 The Bible is a powerful book with a message of hope. What other books have given you hope?

Trailer

Do you believe in angels?

The movie family, PG

Eleven-year-old Roger (Joseph Gordon-Levitt) is a sensitive foster child with two wishes: that he will someday live with a family that loves him, and that his baseball team, the Angels, will win the championship. A group of angels led by Al (Christopher Lloyd) appear to Roger and his teammates, and things begin looking up when Roger relays Al's baseball tips to their manager, George Knox (Danny Glover).

This clip (just over 3½ minutes)

Start 1:17:18

"What's going on Knox?" George Knox walks into the press conference.

Stop 1:20:49 "I've seen it."

George holds a press conference to respond to reports that he's using angels to help his team win. He's ready to dismiss the rumors as nonsense, but when the kids come into the room he decides to tell the crowd what he believes—that the angels and miracles are real. He says that there are times in life when something stronger, higher, maybe even spiritual, happens in athletics. They can call it whatever they like, but something has changed the way the kids are playing ball.

By the Book

Hebrews 1:14, 13:1-2

Where to take it

📺 What made George Knox change his mind and speak up for what he believed? Could you stand up in front of a crowd and speak up for what you believe?

📺 What do you believe about angels? Do you believe there are good and bad (fallen) angels?

📺 Are angels supernatural beings, humans, both, or neither?

📺 Do you think you've ever had an encounter with an angel? What happened?

📺 What are angels sent to do?

📺 Do you think everyone has a guardian angel? Why or why not?

📺 Would you trust an angel? What could you ask an angel to find out if it was a good or a fallen angel?

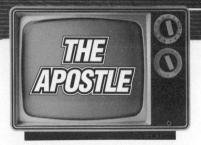

THE APOSTLE

Trailer

Are you prepared to do battle for the Lord?

The movie — drama, PG-13

After Euliss "Sonny" Dewey (Robert Duvall) puts his wife's lover in a coma with a blow from a baseball bat, he changes his name to Apostle E. F. and moves to Louisiana, where he begins working at a local radio station as an engineer. His gift and passion for evangelism is evident when he begins preaching on the radio, on the street—everywhere he goes. He starts a campaign to renovate an old church, hoping to start a revival bigger than anything anyone has ever seen before.

This clip (just under 7 minutes)

Start 1:41:24

Apostle E. F. walks toward the bulldozer with his Bible.

Stop 1:48:09 *After the conversion experience.*

A troubled young man (Billy Bob Thornton), furious that E.F. kicked him out of a church service, returns to the church with four of his buddies and a bulldozer, determined to level the building. E. F. startles him by confronting him with the power of the Holy Spirit and challenges him to drive over the Bible he has placed on the ground. With the congregation praying, E. F. standing firm and confident. The power of God prevails, and the angry man repents on the spot.

By the Book

Romans 1:16; Ephesians 6:10-18

Where to take it

- Where did Apostle E. F.'s confidence come from? Could you treat someone who wanted to destroy you with kindness and compassion?

- How do you think the presence of a television reporter influenced Apostle E. F.'s behavior? If you've ever had a camera on you, how have you behaved (differently/the same/didn't notice)?

- What power does the Word of God have?

- What is significant about each of the body parts God's armor (described in Ephesians 6) protects?

- Which part of your armor is most vulnerable: your belt (truth), breastplate (righteousness), foot coverings (readiness), shield (faith), helmet (salvation), or sword (Word of God)? What can you do to make it stronger?

- What battle are Christians preparing for? How did Jesus use the Word of God as a sword during the Temptation (Matthew 4)?

ARMAGEDDON

Trailer

Have you experienced a father's powerful love?

The movie action/adventure, PG-13

Harry Stamper (Bruce Willis) leads a team of deep core drillers
into outer space to destroy an asteroid the size of Texas that's
heading for Earth. They have only 18 days to stop it from
destroying the world by drilling a hole in it and implanting a
nuclear warhead.

This clip (just over 2 minutes)

Start 2:20:00

> "Houston, do you copy? This is Harry Stamper."

Stop 2:22:05 Grace's hand is on the screen as the
camera pulls back. Harry is on the
surface of the asteroid.

All other plans have failed and time is running out, so Harry
must stay behind to detonate the warhead. He gets a last
chance to say good-bye to his daughter, Grace (Liv Tyler),
and she gets a chance to tell her father she loves him—
something she has always held back. Both Harry and Grace
are honest with each other about their true feelings, knowing
it might be the last chance they have.

By the Book

Ephesians 5:1-2; 1 Peter 1:14-16

Where to take it

What kind of things did Grace tell her father? Is there anything you need to tell your father?

In the past, Grace had said to her dad, "I never want to be like you!" Can you relate? Why do a lot of teens say this to their parents?

What is your relationship with you father like (good/bad/indifferent) and why?

If you could have a different father, who would it be, and why would you choose him?

Is thinking of God as your father difficult for you? Explain.

What has Jesus taught you about the parent-child relationship?

Has your dad ever had to break a promise to you? If so, what was it?

How does someone who hasn't experienced a father's love embrace God as their father? What are some difficulties they might have?

Trailer

Who are you trying to impress?

The movie comedy, PG-13

Mike (Gary Cole) and Carol (Shelly Long) Brady, their six kids, and their housekeeper bring their '70s innocence (as well as their groovy outfits) into the cynical world of the '90s. Aside from the obvious problems that arise with a blended family of this size living under one roof, the Bradys must raise $20,000 in back taxes to save their house.

This clip (just under 3 minutes)

Start 19:33

"Okay troops, time for school."

Stop 22:25   *Jan is in the middle of the road waving to someone who almost hit her.*

Bobby (Jesse Lee) and Jan (Jennifer Elise Cox) need to talk to Dad before he goes to work. Bobby's upset because the kids at school are calling him a fink for being a hall monitor, and Jan thinks she looks like a geek in her glasses. Mike offers them sound advice, but Jan chooses to ignore it. She rides her bike to school without her glasses and narrowly escapes a potentially tragic accident.

By the Book

Matthew 7:1-2; John 7:24; 1 John 2:15-17; Galatians 1:10

Where to take it

📺 What are some reasons the Bradys don't fit in? Should they change, or should society accept them as they are? Do you know anyone who seems to be a misfit? Why do people see them that way, and has anyone taken time to get to know them? Would you?

📺 Describe a time when you felt like you didn't fit in. What did you do about it?

📺 Are you guilty of judging by appearances? In what way (if any) does God want you to judge?

📺 When is it okay to be different? When is it not okay?

📺 Do you pay more attention to what God says about you or what people say about you?

📺 Why is it difficult to earn both the approval of men and of God?

Trailer

Are you willing to die for what you believe in?

The movie epic, R

Based on historical accounts, this film follows the 13th-century Scottish fight for freedom from the tyrannical feudal system of English rule. The battle is led by William Wallace (Mel Gibson), a commoner whose father, brother, and new bride were brutally murdered by the English. Because of their grit and determination, the Scottish successfully defend their homeland from the more powerful and better trained English military.

This clip (over 10 minutes)

Start tape 2, 53:08

William Wallace prays in his cell.

Stop 1:03:13   *Cloth falls from Wallace's hand.*

In this climactic scene, William Wallace has been captured and is awaiting execution for high treason. Alone in his cell, Wallace prays for the strength to die well. He can receive mercy (a quick death) from his executioners if he will kneel and pledge allegiance to the King of England. Wallace refuses to bow and is so gruesomely tortured that even the crowd of onlookers cries for mercy. With his final breath, Wallace screams, "Freedom!" reminding them that his death is not without purpose.

By the Book

Exodus 20:5-6; Matthew 4:8-10

Where to take it

- What religious symbolism did you see in this scene, and what was its significance?

- What message did Wallace convey when he made eye contact with the little child in the crowd?

- Why didn't Wallace struggle against the executioners? He had fought so impressively throughout the movie. Why didn't he go out fighting? Was he giving up?

- What made the crowd change from wanting to see Wallace suffer to wanting mercy for him? Have you ever felt that way about anyone?

- Would you be willing to suffer so much for your beliefs?

- Who in the Bible (besides Jesus) was put to death because of their beliefs?

- Is there something or someone you "bow down to" that God wouldn't approve of?

Trailer

What does divorce cost—besides money?

The movie comedy, PG-13

This is a look at the lives and families of three men in various stages of divorce: Donny (Paul Reiser)—still in love with his ex-wife, trying to relate to his teenage daughter and be a good dad; Dave (Matthew Modine)—unable to make a solid commitment to anyone; and Vic (Randy Quaid)—a bitter, hurt, divorced father. The three men's lives intertwine, revealing the harsh realities of divorce and the struggles they face as they attempt to reconnect with their children.

This clip (over 7 minutes)

Start 1:37:35

"Townsend, no more talking!"

Stop 1:44:45   *"Just love them."*

Vic interrupts a radio talk show, venting the frustrations he's feeling over the reasons for his divorce and the effects it's had on him and his family. His honesty and admission of guilt motivate many people to openly discuss their real feelings about the consequences of divorce.

By the Book

Malachi 2:15-16; Matthew 19:3-9

Where to take it

📺 Is it ever okay to divorce?

📺 Why does God hate divorce?

📺 After his divorce, what did Vic realize he had been missing? What had he failed to give his children and wife?

📺 How has divorce affected you (or a parent, or a friend)?

📺 What do you think are the most common reasons for divorce?

📺 After Donny and Dave opened up to each other, did the way they comforted each other surprise you? Why?

📺 What did you learn from the way Dr. Townsend (the talk show host) handled Vic's initial hostility?

Trailer

Can you put a price tag on friendship?

The movie comedy, PG-13

Ronald (Patrick Dempsey) is tired of being thought of as a geek. He manages to convince one of the most popular girls at school to go out with him for one month if he pays her $1,000. Simply by being with Cindy (Amanda Peterson), Ronald quickly gains friends and status, but as his popularity grows, so, unfortunately, does his ego. He learns a difficult lesson about the importance of being real when his deal with Cindy is exposed.

This clip (just over 3 minutes)

Start 1:12:39

Cindy throws a cup at the stereo and then says, "You!"

Stop 1:15:47

Ronald walks into the shed and lays down to cry as the scene fades.

Ronald's attempt to buy affection and friends has backfired. It's New Year's Eve, and Cindy, tired of being used, lets everyone know that he has paid her to go out with him—he's a phony, and he's tried to buy their friendship. The game's up and the joke's on Ronald. No one wants anything to do with him. Wandering through the streets, he finds himself on the outside looking in at a party in full swing. Alone, in the dark, the tears come.

By the Book

Matthew 16:26; Luke 16:9

Where to take it

- What do you think it means to forfeit your soul? How did Ronald forfeit his soul?

- Would you or have you ever pretended to be something you're not just to be popular? Why?

- What are some of the positive and negative aspects of popularity?

- Contrast worldly wealth with true wealth.

- What do you think makes kids popular? Do you think most of the popular kids at school are happy?

- What do you think Jesus would say to someone who isn't very popular that might help him feel better about himself? Are you willing to do the same?

- How can popularity be used for God's purposes?

Trailer

Are you depending on someone else to define who you are?

The movie comedy, PG-13

It's high school graduation night—time for the biggest party of the year. Amanda (Jennifer Love Hewitt) has just broken up with the captain of the football team and is doing some serious soul-searching, unaware that someone at the party is trying to work up enough courage to tell her how much he cares about her.

This clip (just over 1½ minutes)

Start 45:00

"If you ask me, I never saw you two together in the first place."

Stop 46:39

"I don't think I know me as anything else."

Amanda tells her cousin how great it was dating the captain of the football team, that it was fun being cool and popular. She confesses she dated him for such a long time not only because it made her feel special to be liked by someone so popular, but because she was afraid of being alone. She didn't know who she was without her boyfriend, and now that their relationship is over, she wonders who she really is.

By the Book

John 1:12; 1 John 3:1

Where to take it

- What are the mixed emotions Amanda feels now that she is no longer dating the captain of the football team?

- Why did Amanda's identity change when she was dating him? Has your identity ever changed when you were dating someone?

- Do you know people that don't seem to have an identity separate from their boyfriend or girlfriend? What do you think about that type of relationship?

- How has your sense of identity changed, knowing you are a child of God?

- What did John mean by, "How great is the love the Father has lavished on us"?

- Can you lose your identity in Christ? How have you changed since you've come to know Christ?

- What are the positives and negatives of a strong dating relationship?

Trailer

Is the risk of losing someone worth the joy of loving them?

The movie drama, PG-13

Seth (Nicholas Cage), an angel who is deeply interested in the human condition, becomes attracted to a female doctor, Maggie (Meg Ryan), and gives up immortality to experience the joys and risk the sorrows of love.

This clip (just over 4 minutes)

Start — 1:35:11

Seth is on the couch.

I would rather have had one breath of her hair, one kiss from her mouth, one touch of her hand, than an eternity without it. One."

Stop — 1:39:12

Not only does Seth experience the joys of human love, he learns the pain of loss when Maggie dies. When an angel comes to visit him he questions God's fairness and wonders if he's being punished. The angel asks Seth if he still would have chosen to be human if he had known it was going to hurt so much. Seth says that just one kiss or touch from Maggie would have been better than an eternity without her.

By the Book

Psalm 39:4-5; Matthew 6:19-21; Philippians 3:20

Where to take it

- Does Seth think he made the right decision? Do you think he did?

- Think of a person you risked loving, even though the relationship ended. Was it worth it? Did it make you a better person? How?

- What does it mean to store up treasure in heaven? What kind of treasure is Jesus talking about in Matthew 6?

- Seth gave up immortality to experience love. Is there anything you want so much you would risk giving up your heavenly treasure? Is it possible to lose your heavenly treasure?

- Think about what it means to be a citizen of your country. What does it mean to have your citizenship in heaven (Philippians 3)? How can you be sure that's where your citizenship is?

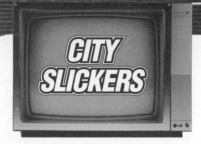

Trailer

Do you remember the best and the worst day of your life?

The movie comedy, PG-13

Mitch (Billy Crystal) is a middle-aged man working at a radio station selling air time to advertisers. Like his friends Phil (Daniel Stern) and Ed (Bruno Kirby), Mitch is suffering from midlife crisis. Feeling like they're missing out on life, the three friends go out west to take part in a cattle drive. As they begin to relax, they find they finally have time to talk about things that really matter.

This clip (just under 2 minutes)

Start 1:13:48

"All right, I got one."

Stop 1:15:47   *"Same day."*

As Mitch, Phil, and Ed ride along the trail, they share intimate details about themselves. Each tries to recall the best and worst days of their lives. Their recollections leave them feeling somber and reflective, as they contemplate sometimes painful childhood memories and the paths they've chosen to follow.

By the Book

Matthew 6:25-34; Ecclesiastes 12:1

Where to take it

📺 Why did these men pick the days they did as their best and worst?

📺 What would you say was the best day of your life? The worst?

📺 Is something from your past robbing you of your joy today?

📺 What memories do you hope to make when you have a family?

📺 How does worrying about our future and dwelling on our past determine whether we remember certain days as good or bad?

📺 What good can come from the bad days we've experienced? Explain.

THE COLOR PURPLE

Trailer

Why does God allow suffering?

The movie drama, R

Based on the novel of the same name by Alice Walker, this film chronicles the life of Celie (Whoopi Goldberg), a young African-American girl growing up in the early 1900s. Fourteen years old and pregnant by her father, Celie struggles not only to survive, but also to break free from the abuse and pain she has suffered all her life.

This clip (just over 3 minutes)

Start 2:04:55

"She'll be back. She got talent."

Stop 2:08:00

"What you do to me, you've already done to yourself."

Celie finally takes a stand against the man who has emotionally and physically abused her for so many years. As she's leaving, she wards off his physical attack with a look of pure hatred. She's ready to face any risks rather than stay and lose what's left of her spirit.

By the Book

John 16:33; Romans 5:3-5; 2 Corinthians 1:3-11

Where to take it

- What do you think Celie meant by, "What you do to me, you've already done to yourself"?

- Why doesn't life automatically get easier when we give everything over to God?

- According to Paul in Romans 5 and 2 Corinthians 1, what are some of the good things that can come from suffering? What are some of the reasons suffering is necessary?

- Is it wrong to be upset or disappointed with God? Have you ever felt that way? Why?

- Why do people stay in abusive or harmful relationships?

- Do you know anyone who is in an abusive relationship? What are some things you can do to help? What are some things you shouldn't do?

Trailer

Can our experiences with God be evidence of his existence?

The movie (science fiction, PG)

Dr. Ellie Arroway (Jodie Foster) has always been convinced of the possibility of extraterrestrial life. Through a series of events, she makes contact with alien life and is told how to construct a spacecraft that would allow more people to meet with them. Billions of dollars later, Arroway's attempts to build the vessel fail. She is accused of misleading the public and must testify at a congressional hearing.

This clip (just under 4 minutes)

▶ **Start 2:19:04**

"Dr. Arroway, you come to us with no evidence, no record, no artifacts."

⏸ **Stop 2:22:54**   "That continues to be my wish."

The government wants physical proof of Dr. Arroway's encounter with aliens, but she has none. She's asked to admit that it never happened, but she can't. She tells them she's had an experience that she can't explain or prove but passionately believes was real. She was given something that changed her forever: a vision of the universe that we're not alone and we belong to something bigger than ourselves. It is her continuing desire that everyone could one day experience the awe, humility, and hope she felt.

By the Book

2 Timothy 3:10-15; Hebrews 11:1-3

Where to take it

- Have you ever been pressured to deny something you really believe? Explain.

- How is Dr. Arroway's experience similar to a conversion experience?

- Why did Dr. Arroway have such a passion for others to share her experience? Do you have a passion for others to have an encounter with Christ?

- Why is it so difficult to believe in something with little or no evidence?

- What kind of evidence do we have of God's existence? What kind of evidence would be convincing to nonbelievers?

- What are some obstacles that keep people from pursuing a relationship with God?

- How would you explain your faith in Christ to someone who doubts Christ even exists?

Trailer

Are you a hero if no one's looking?

The movie comedy, PG-13

When a stroke puts the U.S. President into a coma, his staff decides that the American public should be kept in the dark—so they convince a look-alike comedian (Kevin Kline) to impersonate the president, giving at least the appearance of business as usual. Meanwhile, the First Lady (Sigourney Weaver), also kept in the dark, begins wondering who this man really is.

This clip (over 3 minutes)

⟳ Start 46:00

The street in front of a children's shelter.

◉ Stop 49:07 "*...so just cap 'em and go home.*"

While he and the First Lady are visiting a children's shelter, the "president" spots a boy off in the corner by himself and befriends him. When the ever-present media comes after him for a page-one shot, he criticizes them for trying to exploit quiet, personal moments that should be allowed to remain private and not used for publicity.

By the Book

Matthew 6:1-4; 2 Corinthians 8:8-15

Where to take it

In this scene do you think Dave was being falsely modest? Truly selfless? Indignant? Unrealistic?

What do you think triggered his response to the photographers?

When was the last time you did a truly selfless act of private compassion or devotion and felt the urge to let somebody know what you did? If you told someone, how did it make you feel?

Do you think it's possible for someone to do a compassionate or devotional act without at least a slight desire to let others know about it? Why or why not?

What similarities are there, if any, between the words of Jesus in Matthew 6 and Dave's words to the photographers? Dissimilarities?

DEAD MAN WALKING

Trailer

Can anyone, no matter what they have done, become a child of God?

The movie — drama, R

Sister Helen Prejean (Susan Sarandon) is a nun who receives a desperate letter from death-row inmate, Matthew Poncelet (Sean Penn), a convicted murderer trying to avoid the death penalty. As their relationship develops, Sister Prejean must come to terms with ministering to Poncelet as a fellow child of God despite the horrendous nature of his crimes, while at the same time ministering to the victims' families.

This clip (just under 2½ minutes)

Start 1:35:45

"That boy. Walter."

Stop 1:38:01   *"Thank you for loving me."*

Sister Helen Prejean sits with convicted killer Matthew Poncelet in his cell. When he confesses that he has indeed killed a man, Sister Prejean teaches him that he can become a child of God by asking for forgiveness of his sins and owning up to his responsibility—which he does, realizing that confession doesn't negate what he's done. The best he can do is wish the families peace. Poncelet is grateful for Sister Prejean's compassion and love.

By the Book

1 Timothy 2:3-4; John 6:40, 13:34-35; Luke 5:31-32

Where to take it

📺 Would you be willing to befriend a convicted killer? What was Sister Prejean's motivation?

📺 What difference did Sister Prejean make in Matthew Poncelet's life?

📺 Do you think it's fair that two people, one who spends her life striving for godliness and the other who is a murderer, receive the same reward of heaven? Explain.

📺 Is all sin the same, as God sees it? Are there big sins and little sins? How do most people perceive sin?

📺 What do you think about the death penalty? Is it fair or unfair? Could you condemn someone to death? Why?

📺 Do you agree or disagree with this statement: God desires everyone to be saved.

📺 If a murderer or rapist asked you to forgive them, do you think you could?

Trailer

What legacy will you leave?

The movie *drama, PG*

John Keating (Robin Williams) is a first-year teacher at an all-boys prep school. His intensity and passion inspire his students to love poetry, live for the moment, and challenge convention. His unorthodox teaching methods cost him his job but also radically change the lives of his students.

This clip *(just under 4½ minutes)*

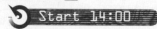

Start 14:00

Students gather in the hallway. "Oh captain, my captain."

Stop 18:22

"Seize the day. Make your lives extraordinary!"

Mr. Keating gathers his English class in the hallway of the school, telling them to look closely at the pictures of the alumni on the wall: all photos of once invincible, hopeful students, now dead. Mr. Keating asks his students what they plan to do with the rest of their lives. He challenges them to seize the day (*carpe diem*), to live every moment to its fullest, and to make their lives extraordinary.

By the Book

John 15:1-8; Luke 12:16-21; Philippians 4:13; James 4:13-17

Where to take it

☐ What are some similarities between Mr. Keating's advice to his students and Jesus' advice in Luke 12? Dissimilarities?

☐ How does the certainty of death affect the way you live?

☐ Where do nonbelievers find significance? Where do you find significance?

☐ If you could do anything without the possibility of failing, what would it be?

☐ What do you want your gravestone to say about you? What do you think people (those who know you well and those who don't) would write about you?

☐ How does *carpe diem* apply to the passage from James 4? How does the meaning differ for a nonbeliever and a believer?

☐ What do you think makes a person successful and extraordinary? Compare and contrast what nonbelievers and Christians consider the marks of a successful life.

Trailer

Why are we so afraid of getting old?

The movie comedy, PG-13

Madeline (Meryl Streep), a self-absorbed Hollywood actress, and Helen (Goldie Hawn) are furiously battling each other: fighting for the love and attention of Ernest (Bruce Willis), fighting over which one of them has the best plastic surgery, and eventually over a cure for aging. It's not until they achieve immortality that they discover life will never be the same again.

This clip [just over 2 minutes]

Start 1:42:20

The two women try to walk out of a pew at the funeral.

Stop 1:44:30

"Do you remember where you parked the car?"

Cadaverous Madeline and Helen attend Ernest's funeral together. As they get up to leave, something the minister says gets their attention. He discloses Ernest's secret of eternal life: giving of himself to others. Madeline and Helen dismiss this information as useless. They leave the church, pull each other down the steps and "fall apart."

By the Book

John 3:16, 14:6, 17:3; Romans 6:23

Where to take it

◻ Why are people afraid to age? Why are they afraid to die? Are you afraid of aging and dying? Explain.

◻ What do you think is the most important thing you can do with your life?

◻ Have you ever known anyone who is obsessed with the way they look? Describe what they consider important.

◻ What makes someone truly handsome or beautiful?

◻ Do you agree or disagree with this statement: It's okay to have nice things, and it's okay to look and feel your best.

◻ What motivates people to have plastic surgery? Do you know anyone who has? Did they look or feel better about themselves after surgery?

◻ What would you like people to say about you at your funeral?

Trailer

If you knew today was your last day, how would you spend it?

The movie drama, PG-13

A mile-wide asteroid is on a direct collision course with Earth. No one knows the extent of the devastation that will take place. Panic spreads at the thought of the end of the world, and plans are made to get as many people as possible into an underground shelter. President Beck (Morgan Freeman) must deliver the devastating news while trying to remain calm so that panic doesn't give way to violence.

This clip (just over 3 minutes)

Start 1:35:03

President Beck's hands on the table.

Stop 1:38:05   *President Beck walks out of the Oval Office.*

NASA has been unable to stop the asteroid or change its course. President Beck addresses the nation, trying to stay calm while explaining the asteroid's imminent impact and what they believe will happen to the planet. A lottery system will be used to determine who will be chosen to live in the underground shelter. People everywhere come to a standstill. Reactions differ, but as the impact of what they've heard sets in, fear begins to spread.

By the Book

John 13:14-17; Luke 22:41, 23:39-43

Where to take it

- If you knew the world was about to end, who would you want to be with? Who would you like to talk to?

- Do you think the lottery system they were planning to use was fair or unfair? Why or why not?

- Name five things you would like to do on your last day.

- Read about Jesus' last day in the book of John. What did he focus on? What instructions did he leave?

- Considering the brevity of life, where should your priorities be focused? What is the greatest priority you should have?

- Are you calm or frantic in a crisis?

- If you could have been with Jesus on his last day, what would you have said to him before he went to the cross?

DUMB AND DUMBER

Trailer

When are you going to grow up?

The movie comedy, PG-13

Harry (Jeff Daniels) and Lloyd (Jim Carrey) are two friends whose intelligence can only be described by the title of the movie. They travel to Aspen, Colorado to return a lost suitcase full of money to its rightful owner, Mary (Lauren Holly).

This clip (just over 2 minutes)

Start 12:18

Lloyd gets Mary's bag out of the car.

Stop 14:37

The airbag explodes in Lloyd's face, and Mary waves good-bye.

As Lloyd drives Mary to the airport, it's painfully obvious that he has developed an enormous crush on her. Since she and Lloyd have only just met, Mary is extremely confused by his sudden outpouring of emotion and his heartbroken reaction to her departure.

By the Book

1 Corinthians 13:11; Ephesians 4:13-15; 1 Peter 2:1-3

Where to take it

📺 Why was Mary trying to get away from Lloyd so quickly?

📺 What childish ways have you given up, and which ones are you not ready to let go of?

📺 How has your thinking and reasoning about God changed since you were a child?

📺 What's the difference between a crush and love?

📺 If you like someone but you're not sure they like you, is it better to tell them how you feel or to not say anything?

📺 What is pure spiritual milk (1 Peter 2:2)? How do we get it? Why do we need it?

📺 Does growing up mean you can't have fun? Name an adult you know who is fun to be around. How do you think they are able to be joyful when they have so many responsibilities?

THE EMPIRE STRIKES BACK

Trailer

Is any problem too big for God to handle?

The movie science fiction, PG

This is the second film of the Star Wars trilogy. Luke Skywalker (Mark Hamill) receives his first training as a Jedi knight while Darth Vader (David Prowse) relentlessly pursues Luke's rebel alliance cohorts, planning to use them as bait, so that he can seduce Luke to the dark side of the Force.

This clip (over 5 minutes)

Start 1:17:01

"Use the Force. Yes. Now the stone. Feel it."

Stop 1:22:12   *"That is why you fail."*

Luke Skywalker travels to Dagobah in search of the Jedi master, Yoda (Frank Oz). Luke knows that to become a Jedi knight he must learn to use the Force. After his X-Wing fighter sinks in the swamp, Luke is instructed by Yoda to lift it out by using the power of the Force. When Luke tries and fails, he gives up and the fighter sinks deeper into the swamp; however, Yoda is successful, telling Luke the reason for his failure is because he does not believe.

By the Book

Philippians 4:13; 2 Timothy 1:7

Where to take it

📺 What was it that Luke didn't believe that caused him to fail?

📺 Can you relate to Luke's lack of faith? Is there something you lack faith in your ability to do?

📺 Compare the Force from Star Wars to God's power. Are there any similarities? Differences?

📺 Can you really do everything like Philippians 4:13 says, or are there limits?

📺 How do we acquire a faith that can move mountains (1Corinthians 13:2)?

📺 Is there anything you need to unlearn so your faith can grow?

FATHER OF THE BRIDE

Trailer

Why is it so hard to let go?

The movie comedy, PG

George (Steve Martin) and Nina (Diane Keaton) are the proud parents of their soon-to-be-wed daughter, Annie (Kimberly Williams). George is the typical nervous father, wanting Annie's wedding day to be special but not quite ready for his little girl to grow up and move away. He discovers just how tiring and expensive "the perfect wedding" can be.

This clip (under 3 minutes)

Start 1:18:57

George opens the front door and looks outside.

Stop 1:21:40

The scene fades as Annie and George hug.

Waking up to the sound of a bouncing basketball, George investigates and finds Annie shooting hoops in the middle of the night. It is the eve of her wedding and she is restless, sensing her whole life is about to change. The bedroom of the house she grew up in will no longer be her home, and while she looks forward to her new life, she's not quite ready to let go. George confides that he is having the same problem. It starts to snow, bringing back happy childhood memories, and they share a very special moment together.

By the Book

Luke 2:19, 2:40-52; Genesis 28:1-29:14; John 2:1-11
There are also some loose references to the themes in the book of Ruth.

Where to take it

☐ Who do you think will have a harder time adjusting after the wedding, George or Annie? Why?

☐ When you move out of your parents' house, what do you look forward to doing? What frightens you? What will you miss the most? Who will you miss the most?

☐ What do you think would be the hardest thing about living on your own?

☐ Can we ever outgrow a father's love? God's love?

☐ Describe some special moments you've had with your mom and dad.

☐ What are some similarities between the mixed emotions Annie was feeling and those of someone who is terminally ill?

☐ Why do you think parents have such a hard time letting their kids grow up?

☐ Is it easy or difficult for you to let go and change?

65

FIELD OF DREAMS

Trailer

Are you serving because you're expecting something in return?

The movie drama, PG

Ray Kinsella (Kevin Costner) hears a voice saying, "If you build it, he will come." Interpreting the voice as an instruction to build a baseball diamond in his corn field, he does, and out of the cornfield come Shoeless Joe Jackson (Ray Liotta) and the rest of the Chicago Black Sox baseball team. Ray continues to hear the voice and seeks the help of author Terrence Mann (James Earl Jones) to decipher the meaning of the field.

This clip (10 minutes)

Start 1:31:00

"Hey, do you want to come with us?"

Stop 1:41:00   *Ray plays catch with his dad.*

When Shoeless Joe invites Terrence into the field of dreams, Ray is furious because he is the one who has sacrificed time, energy, and possibly even his farm to build the baseball diamond. Terrence disappears into the cornfield, excited and ready to take the risk. Ray pleads his case to Shoeless Joe, who questions Ray's motivation for building the field. It's only when Ray resolves to get on with his life that he is permitted a glimpse into the field of dreams in the person of his father, John (Dwier Brown), seen as a young ballplayer in his prime of life.

By the Book

Philippians 2:3-4; Luke 6:31; 1 Corinthians 13:4-5

Where to take it

📺 Why did Ray build the baseball diamond? For himself? For others? Did he even know why?

📺 Does God ever have us create things that benefit others more than ourselves?

📺 Can you relate to Ray's feelings when he wasn't invited into the cornfield? Have you ever not been chosen for something you really wanted to do? Explain.

📺 Why doesn't God give you everything you want?

📺 What qualities do you need to be able to go where and when God calls you?

📺 How can we get rid of selfish ambition?

📺 How can we eliminate the what's-in-it-for-me attitude from what we do?

📺 Do you think heaven really is where dreams come true? Can we build a heaven on earth?

📺 Finish this verse: "Do unto others..." What does it mean to you on a daily basis?

Trailer

How much of a risk are you willing to take to help someone?

The movie drama, PG-13

Forrest Gump (Tom Hanks), a simple man with a low IQ, looks at life with endearing innocence. A series of coincidences puts him in the right places at the right time, and he unwittingly becomes a key player in some of the most crucial events to shape America from the 1950s through the 1970s. Although Forrest encounters some of the most prominent people of those decades, he never forgets his childhood friend, Jenny (Robin Wright), who is his one true love.

This clip (under 2½ minutes)

> ### Start 18:00
> *"It's funny how you remember things and some things you can't."*

> ### Stop 20:23
> *"Jenny and me was like peas and carrots."*

Because of a medical condition, Forrest must wear special leg braces, which only add to the ridicule he faces because of his less-than-average intelligence. As he climbs into the bus on the first day of school, the children sense his uneasiness. No one will let him sit down. Finally, Jenny invites him to share her seat. Forrest will remember this act of compassion for the rest of his life.

By the Book

Luke 10:25-37; Ephesians 4:32-5:2

Where to take it

- What did Jenny risk by defending Forrest? What similarities do you see between her actions and those of the Good Samaritan?

- Have you ever had to choose between standing up for someone or letting someone else take that responsibility? What did you choose and why?

- Why do you think it's so difficult to show kindness to people different from ourselves?

- Luke 10 says, "Love your neighbor as yourself." Who is *your* neighbor?

- The Samaritan in Luke 10 spent two things we are often short of: time and money. Have you ever been late and short of cash, and seen a stranger needing help? What did you do?

- Everyone has different ways of expressing compassion. What are some ways you have expressed compassion for people you know? For strangers?

- According to Ephesians 4:32-5:2, what are some of the character traits God wants you to develop so that you can become more like him?

THE GHOST AND THE DARKNESS

Trailer

Can you defend yourself against the enemy?

The movie adventure, R

Set in Africa in 1898, this film is based on the true story of two lions that killed over 130 people in a nine-month period. Engineer John Patterson (Val Kilmer) is sent to Africa to build a bridge for the railway; however, his large workforce is dwindling as the lions kill more workers. Remington (Michael Douglas), an American big game hunter, is called in by the railroad company to help kill the man-eating lions.

This clip (just over 4½ minutes)

 Start 1:36:41

Shot of full moon with night clouds sweeping over.

Stop 1:41:16   *Remington looks up at John after the lion is killed.*

Patterson, Remington, and an African tribesman are hunting at night for the man-eating lions that have terrorized their work camp. One of the lions leaps out from the bushes to attack John who has fallen from the safety of his hunting stand, but John is able to shoot and wound the lion. As the lion retreats, Patterson and Remington follow it, feeling its eyes on them, hunting them down. The lion leaps out of the bushes, but Remington is able to kill it before it can reach John. The men are visibly shaken but relieved.

By the Book

1 Peter 5:8-9; Ecclesiastes 4:9-10

Where to take it

How is the devil like a roaring lion? (Compare hunting methods of each one and what they do with their victims.)

How can you resist the attacks of the devil?

Is there any sin that challenges your self-control and alertness?

Patterson and Remington feel the lion watching them as they try to stalk it. Who is the hunter and who is the hunted?

Do your friends help you resist the temptation to sin, or are you more tempted to sin when you're with them? Why?

Why is it so hard to resist things that are so momentarily pleasurable?

Trailer

Why isn't just knowing what the Bible says enough?

The movie drama, R

Will Hunting (Matt Damon) is a genius. Well-read and considered an expert on most subjects, he possesses astonishing comprehensive skills and an amazing photographic memory. He also possesses a major character flaw: a complete lack of respect for authority, which leads to trouble with the law. As part of his probation agreement, Will must see Sean (Robin Williams) once a week for therapy. Their sessions reveal that despite Will's mental brilliance, he is an emotionally empty young man.

This clip (just under 3 minutes)

Start 54:37

Sean and Will sit on a park bench. Sean says, "Thought about what you said to me the other day."

Stop 57:30

"I doubt you've ever dared to love anyone that much."

For one of their counseling sessions, Sean takes Will to a park. As great as Will's knowledge is, because he has never fully experienced life, his actions show that he lacks maturity, perception, and sensitivity. Sean explains that there is a vast difference between head knowledge and heart knowledge. Head knowledge can be gained by reading books. Heart knowledge comes from living—and loving. This is where Will's greatest challenge lies.

By the Book

James 1:22, 2:14-16; Luke 6:46-49

Where to take it

- Have you ever had an experience that challenged something you believed in? Did your experience affirm or change your belief? How?

- If you could live the life of any person from the Bible, which would it be and why?

- What have you read about that you would like to experience?

- As you read the Bible and your knowledge of God's Word grows, what are some ways you can put that knowledge to use in your daily life?

- What is the difference between knowing about God and knowing God? How can you be sure you know God?

- Do you agree or disagree with this statement: It's necessary to know a lot about the Bible to have a good relationship with God. Why or why not?

Trailer

When's the last time you made an effort to connect with someone?

The movie drama, PG-13

In this movie about life in the '90s in Los Angeles, an adulterous lawyer tries to reconnect with his wife, a woman discovers an abandoned baby, a Hollywood mogul's attitude changes after being mugged, and a tow-truck driver tries to get his sister out of a dangerous neighborhood. Each struggles to do more than just survive; they try to become decent, moral, caring human beings who aren't afraid to do what's right.

This clip (under 2½ minutes)

🕐 **Start 1:15:02**

"Uh, look, the other night."

🕐 **Stop 1:17:26**

"You're not bothering me. You're just buying me breakfast."

Simon (Danny Glover) and Mack (Kevin Kline) sit in a coffee shop trying to get to know each other. Simon saved Mack's life from a group of gang members and Mack feels indebted; however, Simon insists that Mack owes him nothing. Mack recalls another time when someone stepped in and saved him from an oncoming bus. He regrets not taking the time to get to know her or thank her more than he did. He wonders if she was real or an angel. He wonders the same about Simon.

By the Book

Proverbs 3:27; Matthew 6:1-4; Ephesians 4:29

Where to take it

- Do you think it was easy or difficult for Mack to thank Simon? Is it easy or difficult for you to thank people? Why?

- How do you think Simon felt when Mack thanked him? Is it easy or difficult for you to accept thanks? Why?

- What keeps you from helping people?

- Do you know someone who tells everyone when he does something nice? What does God say about doing good (Matthew 6:1-4)?

- Is Simon an angel? Why do you think that?

Trailer

Can you control your tongue, or does it control you?

The movie comedy, PG

This nostalgic look at the summer loves and school days of Rydell High School reveals that although the 1950s are typically thought of as innocent and fun, the emotions and issues high school kids faced then are surprisingly similar to the ones high school kids face today.

This clip (over 1½ minutes)

Start 1:20:30

Marty walks through the bathroom and says, "Hey Riz."

Stop 1:22:14
Rizzo informs Kenickie the baby is not his.

It seems like everyone from Rydell High is at the drive-in. What's playing on the screen is secondary to who's with whom and who's doing what. Two members of the Pink Ladies (a raucous group of girls with a reputation for being fast and loose) take a trip to the bathroom, where Rizzo (Stockard Channing) informs her friend, Marty (Dinah Manoff), that she might be pregnant but hastily warns her not to tell anyone. Marty promises she won't, but as they leave, Marty demands that the crowd move aside to make way for "the lady with the baby." Word spreads quickly, and by the time Rizzo gets to her car, her boyfriend is waiting for her, determined to find out the truth.

By the Book

Proverbs 10:14, 10:21, 11:12-23, 16:28

Where to take it

Why was it so difficult for Marty to keep Rizzo's secret? Was there anything Marty could have done to slow down or stop the secret from spreading? What are some things you can do or say to stop gossip when it starts?

What are some different ways people react when their reputations are damaged? How do you think Rizzo will deal with her damaged reputation?

Before Marty betrayed Rizzo's secret, they were close friends. Do you think they can ever be friends again? When someone betrays you, what, if anything, can be done to reestablish trust?

What are some of the consequences a rumor-starter faces? What consequences does the person being gossiped about face?

How do the verses from Proverbs contrast the words of a fool with those of a righteous person?

Have you ever been the victim of a false rumor? How have you dealt with it?

Trailer

Are you fully prepared when you accept a dare?

The movie comedy, PG-13

Chet (John Candy) is a big-hearted family man who takes his wife and kids out of the big city to a lakeside getaway. While his family isn't as excited about the adventure as Chet is, they are willing to go along with him to make him happy. Chet's plans for a pleasant vacation begin to fade with the arrival of his obnoxious brother-in-law, Roman (Dan Aykroyd) and his family. Nevertheless, he is determined to try to make the best of it and have a good time.

This clip (over 3 minutes)

Start 55:40

"Uh, yeah, that should do it."

Stop 58:50

Chet walks down the stairs with his wife.

Both families are seated together at a restaurant when Chet hears about the legendary 96er: the biggest steak anyone has ever laid eyes on. If Chet can eat every bite of that steak, everyone at his table eats for free. Urged on by Roman, he decides to try; and even though he manages to do it and feels deathly ill, everyone around him is elated. They had the pleasure of watching, but Chet is stuck with the consequences.

By the Book

1 Corinthians 10:23-24, 10:31, Proverbs 23:20-21

Where to take it

- What motivated Chet to eat the 96er? Was it a sin for him to eat it?

- Have you ever accepted a dare? How would the presence of your friends affect your acceptance? What about the presence of your family?

- How much would you dare to risk for someone else's reputation?

- Describe a time you've taken a dare and regretted it. Did you do it or stop before finishing? Why?

- What does Proverbs list as the dangers of overindulging?

- Can our overindulgences hurt others? How?

- Gluttony doesn't just apply to food. Have your excesses gotten out of control in any other areas?

VACATION CABIN

Trailer

Does the perfect mate really exist?

The movie comedy, PG

Phil Connors (Bill Murray) is a Pittsburgh weatherman who is annually (and reluctantly) sent to Punxsutawney, Pennsylvania, to cover the Groundhog Day celebration. After reporting the groundhog's weather forecast, Phil and his crew head out of town only to be forced to return because of a blizzard. The following morning, Phil discovers it is once again February 2, and he must relive his entire day in the town he has grown to despise.

This clip (just over 1½ minutes)

 Start 44:44

Cut to the scene of Tip Top Café.

Stop 46:19

"I'm really close on this one. Really, really close."

Phil asks his producer, Rita (Andie MacDowell), what she would like out of life. The conversation turns to what qualities she would like in a mate. She describes the perfect man—someone so perfect he couldn't possibly exist. Eager to win her affection, Phil sarcastically tells her he nearly fits her description.

By the Book

Ephesians 5:25-28; Proverbs 12:4, 27:15-16, 31:30

Where to take it

- What kind of things does Rita want in a mate? Do you think she's being realistic?

- What would be your top 10 characteristics for the perfect mate?

- Does the perfect mate exist? Explain.

- What are the differences between what the world looks for in a mate and what God says we should look for?

- Put the Proverbs verses in your own words. Do you think these verses apply to men and women?

- What is the main theme of Proverbs 12:4 and Proverbs 27:15-16?

Trailer

How well do you cope with criticism?

The movie **comedy, PG-13**

Failed hockey player Happy Gilmore (Adam Sandler) discovers his slap shot makes an excellent tee shot, so he trades in his stick for a bag of golf clubs and joins the professional golf circuit. Happy must battle both a rival golfer and his own violent temper to win enough money to buy his grandmother's house from the IRS.

This clip **(just under 1½ minutes)**

Start 22:45

"All right. Remember what I said, eh?"

Stop 24:04   *Chubbs frustratingly dubs his head.*

At his first tournament, Happy makes a great first drive onto the green, but now it's putting time—time for a real challenge. He refuses to listen to his advisor, Chubbs (Carl Weathers), and has to take several shots before making the hole. Frustrated and out of control, Happy takes his anger out on a nearby spectator who dares to criticize his arrogance.

By the Book

James 1:19-20, 4:1-10; Ephesians 4:25-27

Where to take it

- What role did pride play in Happy's loss of temper? Do you lose your temper easily?

- Was Happy more angry at himself (for not listening to Chubbs) or the crowd (for jeering at him)?

- What's the danger in not resolving your anger?

- How well do you handle criticism? Do you ignore it? Welcome it? Dismiss it? How does God tell us to handle it?

- Besides anger, what other emotions can cause problems or lead to sin?

- Describe a time you've blown it because you have refused to listen to good advice and had to admit you were wrong.

Trailer

Do you honor your commitments, or are you controlled by your schedule?

The movie family, PG

Peter Pan (Robin Williams) has left Neverland and finally grown up. He's a merger and acquisitions lawyer—married, with children of his own. His old enemy Captain Hook (Dustin Hoffman) kidnaps Peter's children and takes them to Neverland, knowing Peter will follow. With the help of the Lost Boys and Tinkerbell (Julia Roberts), Peter saves his children and recaptures his youthful spirit.

This clip [4 minutes]

 **Start 2:40**

Peter's phone rings in the theater.

Stop 6:40 *Peter's phone rings at the ballpark.*

Peter has promised his son he'll be at his baseball game, but he's running late, so he sends a coworker to videotape it. While Peter catches a cell phone call, his son catches sight of the camcorder. He loses his focus and motivation and strikes out. Peter arrives long after the game is over, realizing that he, too, has struck out—with his family.

By the Book

Matthew 6:19-24

Where to take it

📺 What was Peter's focus?

📺 How would going to his son's baseball game have made a difference to his son? His family?

📺 How have you let down someone you care about? What can you do to make it right?

📺 Why is it easier to let down people we care about than strangers?

📺 How does spending time with people demonstrate love?

📺 Do you consider yourself a reliable person? Are maturity and reliability related? How?

📺 Compared to your parents, what would you like to do the same? Differently?

📺 Has someone you love ever broken a promise to you? Could she have kept the promise if she wanted to or was the broken promise unavoidable? Did an apology make any difference to you?

Trailer

Do you pray all the time or only when you need something?

The movie drama, PG

Norman Dale (Gene Hackman) arrives in Hickory, Indiana, a small farm town obsessed with basketball. Against everyone's wishes he is hired to coach Hickory's high school team. Although Dale was a failure as a college coach and his methods are considered unconventional, he gains support as the team advances to the state championships.

This clip (under 1½ minutes)

◐ Start 1:21:00

"Call time out. Time out!"

Stop 1:22:20 "Keep your strength in the dribble."

In a crucial game one of the starters is injured. Dale calls a time out for substitution. The sub (#53) is on the sideline, praying intently, and Dale prompts him to get into the game, saying, "I think God wants you to play now, son." He goes in, playing better than he ever has before, and tells Dale the reason is that he can feel the Lord's strength.

By the Book

James 5:13; Philippians 4:6-7; 1 Thessalonians 5:16-18

Where to take it

- Have you ever prayed before a game or in another public setting? How did you feel knowing people were watching? What were their reactions?

- Why does God want us to give thanks in all circumstances?

- Since God knows all our needs, do you agree or disagree that we should pray about specific things? Why or why not?

- What are some ways you can make giving thanks a bigger part of your prayers?

- Do you think it's possible to pray continually? Why or why not?

- What do you do if you are interrupted while you are praying?

- How does praying ease anxiety?

Hope Floats

Trailer

How do you hold on when it seems like there's nothing left to hold on to?

The movie drama, PG-13

After learning that her husband has been unfaithful, Birdee (Sandra Bullock) moves back to her hometown in Texas. While dealing with tremendous personal pain, she must learn to ignore whispered rumors and try to make a new life for herself and her young daughter.

This clip (under 7 minutes)

Start 1:43:28

"Birdee, you're not going to make me feel bad about this."

Stop 1:50:15   *The scene fades.*

Birdee and her husband argue (loudly and in front of their young daughter) about his infidelity and her pain and anger. He has met a woman and wants to start a new life. Birdee tells him to go and says that the best part of him is their daughter—at least that much she will always have. Terrified of losing her father, the little girl tries to go with him, but he tells her he is starting a new life and she can't come. Although she is persistent, he drives away. Her father's rejection is devastating. Birdee quietly picks up her heartbroken child, saying nothing, just holding her and letting the tears flow.

By the Book

Romans 8:37-39; John 10:28-30

Where to take it

📺 What are some issues children who come from a divorced family face? Do you see any differences between children who come from divorced homes and those who don't?

📺 Why do children from divorced homes have to work extra hard to have healthy marriages?

📺 According to Romans 8 and John 10, how does a relationship with Jesus bring security to children who are suffering the effects of divorce?

📺 Do you prefer your parents to argue in front of you or take their argument to a private place? Why?

📺 What are some things society promotes and glamorizes that make adultery and divorce more acceptable?

📺 What do you think causes people to cheat on their spouses?

📺 Do you think the tradition of marriage has changed from what God designed, and if so, have the changes been for better or for worse?

📺 Is God asking too much when he asks people to live with and love someone for the rest of their lives?

📺 What characteristics are you looking for in the person you marry?

📺 What do you want to be include in your marriage vows?

Trailer

How far are you willing to step out in faith?

The movie   action, PG

Indiana Jones (Harrison Ford) and his father, Dr. Jones (Sean Connery), are reunited as they embark on a quest in search of the Holy Grail, Jesus' cup from the Last Supper. It has been Dr. Jones' lifelong ambition to possess this legendary relic. They reach its hiding place, only to discover that actually getting to the grail will be no easy task.

This clip   (just under 7 minutes)

Start 1:47:59

"The grail is mine, and you're going to get it for me."

Stop 1:52:19   *"I knew you'd come. My strength has left me."*

Shot and injured by Nazis who also desire the grail, Dr. Jones' survival depends on Indy reaching the grail first. (Legend claims that drinking from the grail brings eternal life.) To get to the grail, Indy must pass three tests: he must become a penitent man (a humble man who kneels before God), he must follow the Word of God, and he must take a step of faith. He passes the first two tests, but with time running out, Indy must summon all his courage, step out in faith and cross an impossibly wide ravine. On the opposite side lies the grail.

By the Book

Luke 8:43-48; Matthew 14:25-31

Where to take it

📺 If you were facing impossible odds and circumstances, could you step out in faith and totally trust God? Have you ever had to?

📺 What were some of the fears Indy had when he looked across that ravine?

📺 What are some situations that have caused you to fear and to doubt God? When? Why?

📺 Compare and contrast the steps of faith the bleeding woman (in Luke 8) and Peter (in Matthew 14) took. What motivated them? What was Jesus' reaction? What was the outcome? What did each of them learn from their experience?

📺 The woman and Peter both demonstrated courage and faith. Name some other people from the Bible who showed faith and trust in God.

📺 Are you in any situation that requires you to take a step of faith and totally trust God? Is there anything that's stopping you?

Trailer

How much of your heart do you put into your relationships?

The movie drama, R

Supertalented sports agent Jerry Maguire (Tom Cruise) starts to have serious doubts about the morality of his job, the company he works for, and the professional sports industry in general. Because of his crisis of conscience, he is fired and starts a new agency assisted only by Dorothy (Renée Zellweger), a secretary from his former company. The new agency has a slow start—their only client being a cocky, unpredictable football player.

This clip (just over 4½ minutes)

Start 1:54:04

"I want you to know I'm about personal attention."

Stop 1:58:36   *"If this is empty, this doesn't matter."*

Jerry and Dorothy take a long, honest look at their relationship. Jerry just doesn't understand what Dorothy wants, which is the "full package." She needs to be loved. Being liked by him isn't enough, and although it hurts, she ends their relationship.

By the Book

1 Corinthians 13:4-8; John 15:13

Where to take it

📺 Is it possible to like someone and then fall in love with them later, or does the love have to be there from the start? Do you believe in love at first sight?

📺 How did Jesus give all his heart and soul when he was on earth?

📺 Would you stay in a marriage or relationship if you felt you were just liked? What would God want you to do? What could you do to make the situation better?

📺 1 Corinthians 13 is called the Love Chapter. Which part of the definition of love describes you the best? In which area do you need improvement?

📺 What are three things important to a healthy marriage?

📺 Did Jerry love Dorothy or did he mistake some other strong emotions for love? Has that ever happened to you?

Trailer

Do you trust God even when life doesn't make sense?

The movie — action, PG-13

Daniel (Ralph Macchio) finds life in California very different from New Jersey and is having a hard time making new friends. The kids don't like his accent, and they don't like outsiders. Daniel tries to stay out of trouble, but several kids from a karate school eventually corner him and beat him up. He seeks help from an elderly gardener named Mr. Miyagi (Pat Morita), wanting to learn karate not for self-discipline, but for self-defense. As his lessons progress, Daniel learns that there is much more to karate than physical skill.

This clip (just over 3 minutes)

Start 1:15:03

Mr. Miyagi says, "Daniel-Son. Come here!"

Stop: 1:18:08 After they bow, Mr. Miyagi says to Daniel, "Come back tomorrow."

Mr. Miyagi has agreed to teach Daniel karate; however, after several days of hard work, Daniel is frustrated and storms off. Mr. Miyagi calls him back and explains why he made Daniel paint the fence, wax the car, and sand the floors. In doing seemingly menial tasks, Daniel had actually been learning the basic movements and foundations of karate. Daniel is appropriately humbled and ready to study. Mr. Miyagi begins his first lesson, stressing that respect must go both ways between student and teacher.

By the Book

Luke 6:46-49; Proverbs 3:5-6

Where to take it

📺 Why was Daniel so upset with Mr. Miyagi?

📺 How do you think Daniel felt at the end of his lesson? What changed his attitude?

📺 Why is it so important to learn the fundamentals of a new skill before attempting it?

📺 What were some of the character traits of Mr. Miyagi that made him a good teacher? What made Jesus a great teacher?

📺 What foundation is your life based on? What are the strengths and weaknesses of this foundation?

📺 Do you trust God with your life even though you may not understand everything he asks? When has this frustrated you? What benefit came from this trust?

Trailer

What if everyone got exactly what they deserved?

The movie drama, PG-13

Based on the classic French novel by Victor Hugo, this is the saga of Jean Valjean (Liam Neeson), imprisoned for 19 years for stealing bread to feed his sister's family. Valjean longs to escape his past and start over, but the world does not readily accept ex-convicts, and he faces rejection everywhere he goes. Shadowed by a police officer named Javert (Geoffrey Rush), Valjean is constantly reminded that his past is far from forgotten.

This clip (just under 7 minutes)

Start 12:35

"You can't sleep here."

Stop 19:33   *The scene fades.*

In the middle of the night, a bishop is startled by a knock at his door. Exhausted and starving, Valjean asks for food and is invited inside. Valjean is given a place to sleep; however, bitter memories of his past flood his mind, and he is unable to rest. He leaves, taking the bishop's silver with him. When Valjean is caught and brought back to the bishop, the bishop not only denies the charges but also reminds Valjean of silver he "forgot" to take. The bishop doesn't condemn Valjean; he reminds him of his promise to become a new man. Valjean's life must begin from this moment on.

By the Book

Luke 15:11-31, 23:39-43; 2 Corinthians 5:17

Where to take it

- Would your initial response to Valjean have been more like the bishop's or the old woman's? Why do you think each of them acted the way they did?

- Would you say you're more trusting or skeptical of strangers? Why?

- Why was the bishop so forgiving after Valjean had beaten him and stolen from him? Could you have been as forgiving?

- What are the similarities between what the bishop did for Valjean and what Jesus did for us?

- Why did Valjean go back to his old ways even after he was shown so much kindness? Have you ever been forgiven for something but have gone right back and done the same thing you swore you'd never do? Explain.

- What is unconditional love (see Luke 15)? Who do you know that needs to be shown unconditional love?

- Is there anything you've done that you feel no one, even God, could forgive you for?

- In you own words, define mercy, grace, trust, and redemption.

Trailer

Is it ever okay to lie?

The movie comedy, PG-13

Fletcher Reede (Jim Carrey) is a fast-talking attorney and the world's greatest liar. He has mastered the art of telling people what they want to hear. Fletcher's trouble begins when his son, Max (Justin Cooper), makes a wish that his dad would stop lying for 24 hours. His wish comes true, and Fletcher discovers that his biggest asset (his smooth-talking tongue) has suddenly become his biggest liability.

This clip (just over 1½ minutes)

 Start 9:29

"I can't do it."

Stop 11:03

Fletcher makes a face after the man with a pimple on his nose walks away.

Fletcher brings Max to work with him, and on the way to his office, Fletcher's subtle sarcasm keeps him a step ahead of everyone he encounters. By the time people realize they've been insulted, Fletcher has already moved on.

By the Book

James 3:7-12; Exodus 20:16; Leviticus 19:11

Where to take it

- Do you think it's okay to lie if someone would be hurt by the truth?

- Is keeping silent in the face of injustice the same as lying?

- What, if anything, is the difference between wit and sarcasm?

- If lying promoted something good (like smuggling Bibles), would it be acceptable? Are there any situations when it's acceptable to lie?

- What damage can lies do? How does a lie affect the liar? The person being lied about? The person being lied to?

- Why would it be hard to be honest for an entire day?

- What value is placed on honesty and truthfulness in our society?

Trailer

Are there good reasons for rules?

The movie family, G

Simba is a young lion cub enjoying life and already showing promise as next in line to rule his father's kingdom. However, his youthful exuberance and mischievous nature land him in situations that prove he is far from ready to take on the responsibilities he will have when he is the lion king.

This clip (just under 6½ minutes)

Start 29:10

"This is it. We made it."

Stop 35:33

"Cause nobody messes with your dad. Come here, you."

Lured by the prospect of adventure and the thrill of taking a risk, Simba and his best friend, Nala, wander out of their territory in search of the forbidden elephant burial ground. Fully aware of the danger and their disobedience, they try to convince each other otherwise. Their adventure turns to terror as they are chased by three hungry hyenas. Luckily Simba's father, Mufasa, rescues them, and although Mufasa is angry, he confesses that his biggest fear was the possibility of losing Simba.

By the Book

1 John 2:3-6; Ephesians 6:1-3

Where to take it

- Simba and Nala deliberately disobeyed their parents and found themselves in danger. Have you ever been in a dangerous situation because you've disobeyed your parents? Have your parents ever had to rescue you?

- Do you think the rules your parents have for you are fair? Do you think rules need to change? Why? When? What are some things you can do to see if your family's rules are fair and appropriate?

- What does honoring your parents mean to you?

- How does being obedient show that you love your parents and you love God?

- Mufasa confessed his fear to Simba. Have your parents ever told you their fears? (You don't need to reveal the fears.) If yes, how did knowing their fears change you?

- Have you ever felt indestructible? What made you feel that way? Were you with your friends or by yourself?

- Has anyone ever talked you into doing something you regretted later on? What happened, and what did you learn?

- Do friends make a difference in how you feel about yourself and what you say and do? How?

- It's easy to be obedient when your parents are watching. Do you obey their rules when there's no chance of them ever knowing whether you are obeying?

MADONNA: TRUTH OR DARE

Trailer

Do you see death as an ending or a beginning?

The movie music/documentary, R

This documentary follows pop icon Madonna on her 1990 Blond Ambition concert tour. The backstage view of Madonna is sometimes very different from what we see in her onstage performances. The intimate scenes reveal many different aspects of her complicated personality.

This clip (just over 3 minutes)

> **Start 56:37**
>
> *"Little girl, don't you forget her face laughing away your tears when she was the one who felt all the pain."*

> **Stop 59:55**
>
> *"Can't kiss her good-bye, but I promise to try."*

On one of the stops of her tour, Madonna visits her mother's grave and talks about how her mother's death has affected her. She was only four when her mother suddenly died, and no one explained the reasons to her. Madonna wonders how her mother could have died so young (since she was such a religious woman) and also wonders if she did something wrong to have her mother taken away from her. She lies on the ground, next to her mother's grave, clearly still struggling with these questions.

By the Book

John 14:1-4; Isaiah 57:1-2; Psalm 116:15

Where to take it

What are some struggles and questions a nonbeliever has when they think about death?

What is different about the Madonna in this scene and the one you usually see in videos? How does this scene help you understand Madonna better?

How did her mother's death affect Madonna? Do you know anyone who lost their mother at a young age? How has it affected them?

Why do people view death so negatively if these verses speak of hope and peace?

What hope do these three verses give concerning death?

MALICE

Trailer

Who are you praising more, God or yourself?

The movie   mystery/suspense, R

A New England college professor and his wife, Tracy (Nicole Kidman), are happily married and planning to have children someday. Their dreams are shattered when Tracy is taken to the hospital and operated on by Dr. Jed Hill (Alec Baldwin), a surgeon with an enormous reputation (and an ego to match).

This clip   (just over 5 minutes)

Start 1:01:15

A woman opens a door to a room full of lawyers and doctors.

Stop 1:06:25   *"This side show is over."*

During an inquiry into Tracy's surgery, it is revealed that, although Dr. Hill had a reputation as a brilliant doctor, he was not appointed Chief of Staff due to his "God-complex." Dr. Hill, cold and calculating, goes off the record, admitting that he does indeed have a God-complex, even going so far as to equate himself with God. His arrogance is powerful enough to shock the room into silence.

By the Book

Romans 12:3; Mark 9:35; Proverbs 16:5, 27:2

Where to take it

📺 Do you find Dr. Hill appealing? Frightening? What words would you use to describe him?

📺 How would you define a God-complex?

📺 Can you name someone from the Bible who had a God-complex? What effect did it have on his life and the plans God had for him?

📺 Is pride a sin? Why or why not?

📺 How can power be used for good in the secular world?

📺 What did Jesus mean by the phrase "servant of all"?

📺 What talents or abilities has God given you that could cause arrogance? What can you do to keep your pride under control?

Trailer

How well are you prepared to face your problems?

The movie action, PG-13

Don Diego de la Vega's (Anthony Hopkins) alter ego is Zorro, a black-masked protector who fights evil and defends helpless peasants against the corrupt nineteenth century Mexican government. Don Diego has spent many years in prison and returns to avenge his wife's murder and save his daughter from his archenemy, Don Rafael Montero (Stuart Wilson II). The prison years have taken their toll, so Don Diego asks Alejandro Murrieta (Antonio Banderas) for help. He sees Murrieta has courage and wit and trains him to become the next Zorro.

This clip (3½ minutes)

 Start 51:00

Zorro falls off of his horse and is surrounded.

Stop 54:30

Zorro runs out of the burning building just as it explodes.

The younger Zorro is breaking in a difficult horse that suddenly goes out of control and crashes through the stable walls into a barracks of Mexican soldiers. Zorro is surrounded by dozens of attackers, and although the odds are against him, he knows he has the training and ability to outwit them and escape. He single-handedly defeats every soldier, and as the frightened men scatter, Zorro pauses to savor his victory, narrowly escaping a deadly explosion.

By the Book

1 Corinthians 10:13; 1 John 4:4; 2 Timothy 1:7

Where to take it

📺 Do you think Zorro was scared or confident in this situation? Is it possible to be both frightened and confident at the same time?

📺 Where did Zorro's confidence come from?

📺 What confidence can we gain from reading 1 Corinthians 10:13? From 1 John 4:4?

📺 Which is more difficult: believing these verses are true or acting upon the belief that they are true? Why?

📺 How can we develop our confidence in God?

📺 What mistake did Zorro make at the end of this scene that nearly cost him his victory?

Trailer

Do you want to be part of God's big picture?

The movie · action/comedy, PG-13

Agents Kay (Tommy Lee Jones) and Jay (Will Smith) are members of the Men in Black, a top secret government organization dedicated to policing and monitoring alien activity on the earth. When an alien "bug" comes to New York City, kills two extraterrestrial dignitaries, and steals a galaxy, it's up to Kay and Jay to exterminate it and save the planet.

This clip (just under 1½ minutes)

Start 1:11:48

An old man and a dog at a booth.

Stop 1:13:19

"If the galaxy's here, it's not in Orion's belt."

Jay and Kay are in a desperate race to track down the stolen galaxy. Searching for information, the Men in Black interrogate an alien (disguised as a dog), who is quick to point out just how limited Jay and Kay's understanding of the universe really is.

By the Book

Job 42:2-3; Ephesians 3:17-19

Where to take it

- Why doesn't God completely reveal how he works? If God did try to explain it to us, would we be able to understand? Do you think we'll ever understand?

- Have you ever tried to count the stars in the sky at night? How does it make you feel when you compare your size to the size of the universe?

- Considering how big the universe is, how big do you think God is?

- Do you believe in aliens or extraterrestrial life? Does the Bible have anything to say on this subject?

- What are some things that limit our understanding of God?

- Read Ephesians 3:1. Describe the love of Christ in your own words (make it personal).

MIRACLE ON 34TH STREET (1994)

Trailer

Is seeing believing?

The movie family, PG

In this remake of the 1947 holiday classic, Dorey Walker (Elizabeth Perkins) is an executive for Macy's Department Store in search of a new Santa. She hires a man named Kris Kringle (Richard Attenborough) who insists he is the real Santa Claus. Naturally, many people are skeptical, including Dorey and her daughter, Susan (Mara Wilson). Susan comes to believe Kris, but when he is charged with mental instability, he has to go to court to prove his identity.

This clip (just under 4 minutes)

Start 1:35:20

"All rise."

Stop 1:39:07 *"Case dismissed."*

Susan confidently approaches the judge and gives him a handmade Christmas card. "In God We Trust" is circled on the dollar bill she has placed inside. The judge smiles and wishes the courtroom a merry Christmas, saying that if the government says it trusts God without physical proof, the state of New York can accept Santa's existence in the person of Kris Kringle.

By the Book

Hebrews 11:1; Mark 11:22-24; 2 Corinthians 4:18, 5:7

Where to take it

- What is blind faith? Have you ever had to rely on something completely in blind faith?

- Susan was confident as she approached the judge's bench. How can you feel confident when people are skeptical about your beliefs?

- Why do you think "In God We Trust" is printed on our currency? Do you think most Americans today believe and live by this phrase?

- How can we focus more on the eternal instead of the temporary? Is anything taking your focus off what will last for eternity?

- What's the difference between living by faith and living by sight?

- What do believers put their faith in? Nonbelievers?

- How would you explain your faith to a nonbeliever?

Trailer

Are you having trouble putting your problems in perspective?

The movie comedy, PG

Like most young couples, Walter (Tom Hanks) and Anna (Shelly Long) dream of owning their own home. They can't find anything they can afford until Walter's real estate buddy tells them about a great bargain. They realize the price was too good to be true when they move in and the staircase falls apart. As their house slowly crumbles around them, so does their dream—and their marriage.

This clip (just over 3 minutes)

 Start 39:00

"Hi, this is Julia Childs."

Stop 42:03   *Walter laughs uncontrollably after the bathtub falls through the ceiling.*

Walter and Anna are struggling to fix up their new home, but things are breaking faster than they can be repaired. Faulty plumbing forces Walter to boil water on the stove for Anna's bath, but as he waits, faulty wiring causes each kitchen appliance to self-destruct, ending with the explosion of the stove. He salvages enough water for Anna, but when he pours it, the tub crashes through the floor. Struck by the absurdity of their situation, Walter collapses in a heap of hysterical laughter, knowing that it's only a matter of moments before the next catastrophe strikes.

By the Book

James 1:2-3; 1 Corinthians 10:13

Where to take it

- Why does Walter laugh hysterically when his dream house is crumbling around him? How would you have reacted?

- Are you more patient than you were as a little child? Less? Are your parents patient? What are some things that cause you to lose patience?

- Describe a time when you totally lost your temper in an intense circumstance. Did you feel better or worse after venting your anger? Did it change the situation? How?

- How easy is it for you to laugh at yourself when things don't go the way they're supposed to?

- What do you think about considering it "pure joy" when you face trials?

- Does knowing that God will not give you anything you cannot handle make you afraid or give you comfort?

- You've probably never had a day as bad as Walter's, but have you had one that's come close (as far as testing your endurance)? Describe that day, and if you were able to laugh about it at the time. Can you laugh about it now?

Trailer

How will the legacy you're leaving be measured?

The movie   drama, PG

Frustrated composer Glenn Holland (Richard Dreyfus) accepts a teaching job at a high school, hoping that someday he will write music for which he will be remembered and loved. It isn't until he retires that he realizes his success hasn't been measured by riches or fame but by the number of lives he has touched.

This clip   (just under 8 minutes)

Start 2:11:40

"Now what is that?"

Stop 2:19:25   *Mr. Holland conducts his symphony.*

Mr. Holland enters the auditorium, realizing a celebration has been planned to honor him. Deeply moved, he begins to see how many students he has influenced, how many lives he has touched. He is given a gift: he is asked to conduct a specially assembled orchestra (composed of former students) in the symphony he has worked on most of his life. It is the crowning achievement of his career to see that his legacy is much more than notes on paper. His students are his symphony; the melodies and notes of his opus are the music of his life.

By the Book

Matthew 7:16-20

Where to take it

- What was the legacy Mr. Holland was leaving? What was his success measured by?

- In your own words, what does it mean to leave a godly legacy?

- What does Jesus mean by bearing fruit? What is good fruit? Bad fruit?

- What did you want to be when you were younger? What do you want to be now?

- How are you using your gifts and talents for God's kingdom?

- What can you do to encourage people who are using their gifts and talents but aren't getting much recognition right now?

- Have you ever had a teacher who greatly impacted your life? Have you told them? Would you be willing to, knowing it would encourage them?

Trailer

Do you have a hard time admitting you're wrong?

The movie comedy, PG-13

Julianne (Julia Roberts) doesn't realize she's in love with her best friend, Michael (Dermot Mulroney), until he calls to tell her that he's getting married in four days. Convinced that he's marrying the wrong woman, she flies to Chicago on the pretense of helping him with wedding preparations, but her plans are to rekindle their romance.

This clip (just over 3 minutes)

Start 1:32:26

Head shot of Julianne walking toward Michael.

Stop 1:35:32   *"Well, that part I knew."*

At the risk of ruining their friendship, Julianne confesses to Michael that she loves him and that all she wanted was to stop him from marrying Kimmy (Cameron Diaz). Julianne is brutally honest with Michael and with herself. She acknowledges that her obsession has driven her to terrible lengths but knows it doesn't excuse what she's done. At first, Michael is shocked and angry, but he accepts her apology and offers her his forgiveness, thanking her for loving him that much.

By the Book

Matthew 18:21-22; Colossians 3:13

Where to take it

📺 Why was Michael so understanding and quick to forgive?

📺 Would you have been forgiving if someone tried to ruin your wedding, your graduation, or any other special event in your life?

📺 If you were Kimmy, how forgiving would you be of Julianne? Of Michael?

📺 Have you ever confessed your shortcomings to your best friend? How did she react?

📺 Do you agree or disagree with this statement: You can't date your best friend, and you can't marry your best friend.

📺 Does forgiveness come easy for you? Why or why not?

📺 Is it possible to be best friends with someone of the opposite sex?

📺 What is obsessive love? Is it genuine love or some other emotion?

NINE MONTHS

Trailer

Are you ready to take responsibility for your actions?

The movie — comedy, PG-13

Sam (Hugh Grant) seems to have it all: a great car, a good job, and a beautiful girlfriend, Rebecca (Julianne Moore). When she tells him she's pregnant, his reaction is anything but what she'd hoped for. Sam knows he needs to accept responsibility for his actions, but first he must conquer his panic and fear.

This clip (just over 3 minutes)

Start 15:55

A red Porsche drives down the road.

Stop 19:05 *Rebecca's unhappy face.*

While out for a drive on a beautiful sunny day, Rebecca tells Sam she's pregnant with his child. Sam is so shocked, they crash, but luckily neither of them is hurt. He asks Rebecca if she's 100 percent positive. She'd like his attitude to be more positive! He blames the pregnancy on her, insinuating that she deliberately chose not to use birth control. Seeing how unprepared Sam is to accept his share of responsibility, Rebecca is deeply and bitterly disappointed and unsure of their future together.

By the Book

1 Thessalonians 4:3-8

Where to take it

📺 Describe Sam's reaction to Rebecca's news and Rebecca's response to his reaction.

📺 What do you do when someone doesn't respond the way you want them to? What about when God doesn't respond the way you expect?

📺 Why did God give us guidelines for sex? Why does the Bible instruct us to avoid sexual immorality?

📺 Do you know anyone who's had a baby without the support of a husband? What struggles did she have during the pregnancy and after the birth?

📺 What are some of the consequences that come from poor sexual choices? What do you think is the most effective thing kids could hear or see that would help them realize these consequences are real?

📺 Why do you think the film industry, for the most part, depicts the pleasures of sex while ignoring the consequences?

Trailer

Are you thriving or just surviving?

The movie comedy, PG-13

The Buckmans have all the trappings of a large family, including estranged relatives, overachievers, black sheep, divorced and single parents, eccentrics, and rebellious teenagers. Gil (Steve Martin) is at the center of it all: the conservative son, brother, and father; trying to please everyone at once and turn conflict into peace while searching for his own identity and purpose in life.

This clip (just under 7 minutes)

Start 1:49:45

"I love you."

Stop 1:56:40   *Gil hugs his wife.*

When Grandma (Helen Shaw) talks no one listens, because most of the family assumes she's senile. She actually has a lot to say, and in this scene, she describes the difference between two attractions at an amusement park: the merry-go-round and the roller coaster. She explains that a lot of people choose the ease of the merry-go-round since there isn't any challenge involved in riding it. She, on the other hand, would choose the roller coaster because the ups and downs are much more exciting than just going around. Gil misses the point, hearing the words but not the wisdom—that most people choose the safe, easy route, but the few risk takers who welcome the ups and downs of life get the most out of living.

By the Book

John 10:10; Mark 8:35

Where to take it

📺 Which ride best resembles your life, the merry-go-round or the roller coaster?

📺 Do you think it's possible to have both consistency and predictability and adventure and excitement?

📺 Who is the thief in John 10:10? How does he steal, kill, and destroy? What does he want?

📺 What does Jesus mean by "life to the full"?

📺 How can you save your life by losing it? Isn't that a contradiction? What does it mean?

📺 Do you remember a time when you should have taken a risk but held back out of fear?

📺 Name five fears that are keeping you from achieving your dreams.

PEE WEE'S BIG ADVENTURE

Trailer

Do you start your day with a healthy dose of God?

The movie   comedy, PG

Pee Wee Herman (Paul Rubens) is an adult perpetually stuck in childhood. Like most children, his priorities revolve around his possessions. His beloved bike is missing, and he is willing to risk anything to find it. He leaves his safe, familiar surroundings and sets off on the biggest adventure of his life.

This clip (over 4½ minutes)

Start 3:36

Pee Wee wakes up in his bed.

Stop 8:24   *Pee Wee leaves the breakfast table.*

Pee Wee wakes up from a wonderful night's sleep and goes through his morning routine: jumping on the bed, putting on his rabbit slippers, playing with his toys, getting dressed, and cooking breakfast for himself. Pee Wee, it seems, is his own best friend.

By the Book

1 Timothy 4:8; Mark 1:35; Joshua 1:8

Where to take it

- How does spending time with God strengthen you for the day ahead?

- Do you spend time alone with God on a regular basis? What makes it most difficult for you? How could you make it easier?

- Why do you think Jesus prayed early in the morning?

- What tools are available to help build your spiritual relationship with God? Which ones are you using and which are gathering dust?

- Are there any times during your morning, daytime, or evening routines that could be used for prayer time?

- What habits do you need to develop that might improve the condition of your relationship with God?

123

Trailer

Have you considered how what you say and the way you say it affects those around you?

The movie   comedy, R

Two businessmen trying to get home in time for Thanksgiving are delayed by the effects of a fierce winter storm. Continually thrown together through a series of comic mishaps, Neil (Steve Martin) and Del (John Candy) find themselves struggling to maintain civility as their very different personalities collide. Rigid, uptight Neil is irritated by Del's endless eccentricities, and tension escalates as their initial politeness and patience wears thin and their true feelings about each other surface.

This clip   (2 minutes)

▶ **Start 28:20**

"You're no saint."

◀ **Stop 31:20**   "What you see is what you get."

After a long, exhausting day, Neil is at the end of his rope. Not only does he have to share a hotel room with Del, they have to share the same bed! The noises Del makes as he tries to get comfortable are too much for Neil. His anger and frustration boil over, and he unleashes a torrent of words that catch Del completely off guard. Clearly wounded, Del considers what has been said and tells Neil that, although he knows he is far from perfect, he has no intention of changing. Realizing the extent of the damage he has done, Neil feels miserable, knowing his words can never be taken back and the pain he has inflicted may never completely heal.

By the Book

Proverbs 12:18, 15:1-4, 21:23; James 3:7-10

Where to take it

Do you think Neil's criticisms were justified? Why or why not?

What are some things Neil could have done to avoid getting so angry that he couldn't control what he said? What are some things you do when you feel anger building up inside?

Why do you think Dell didn't respond to Neil's criticism with angry words of his own? The last time someone criticized you, either justly or unjustly, how did you react?

What caused Neil to realize he had gone too far? Describe how you feel when you go too far and say things that you can't take back.

What are some situations or circumstances that can cause an otherwise in-control person to have an out-of-control tongue?

Do you think people would say that the words you speak build people up or tear them down? Why? Do your words accurately reflect who you are?

What experiences have you had that have radically impacted the way you talk to people (either positively or negatively)?

Is there anyone who makes it difficult for you to speak to people the way you want to—the way you know you should? Without specifing who, explain.

125

Trailer

Does anyone know the real you?

The movie drama, PG-13

Jeremy (Sean Patrick Flannery), or Powder as he is nicknamed (because of his pale skin), is a teenage boy who has been kept in seclusion in his grandfather's basement because of his unusual appearance and mysterious powers: the ability to move objects just by thinking about them and the ability to read people's minds and feelings. Once he is released from isolation, he is treated as an outcast. People are troubled by this different young man and his ability to see into their hearts.

This clip (just under 5 minutes)

Start 1:26:00

A town carnival.

Stop 1:30:59 *Jeremy and Lindsey kiss.*

Powder tries to explain what his life is like to Lindsey (Missy Crider), one of the few people in town to befriend him. He tells her that disconnection and separation are feelings that are taught and that there's no reason to hide emotions or to lie. He can see people's true feelings. Lindsey touches his hand and feels his thoughts: the experiences and feelings that shaped him. She sees past his appearance and into his heart.

vulnerability, being yourself,
being real, connecting with someone,
outward versus inward appearance

By the Book

Matthew 7:1-3; 1 Samuel 16:7

Where to take it

- Do you agree or disagree with Powder's belief that separation (disconnection) is taught? Are we all connected to each other in some way? How?

- What do you think would happen if we could see inside each other and no one could hide the truth?

- Have you ever been ridiculed for expressing your thoughts truthfully? Would you still do it, knowing you might be ridiculed again?

- If you were to play a game with your closest friends where everyone had to be totally honest about what they thought of you and you of them (the good and the bad), would you play? Why or why not?

- Why do people judge by outward appearances? What are they looking for? Why does God look at the heart? What is he looking for?

- Does it bring you hope or worry to know that God is looking at your heart? Is there anything you're ashamed for God to see?

- How judgmental are you? Are you fairly consistent or do your moods affect how critical you are?

Trailer

Who are you more confident in: yourself or God?

The movie action/comedy, PG

This is a fairy tale about the love and adventures of two childhood sweethearts, Westley (Cary Elwes) and Buttercup (Robin Wright). Fearing Westley has been killed, Buttercup reluctantly agrees to marry the odious Prince Humperdinck (Chris Sarandon), but before they are wed, three mercenary villains kidnap her and hold her for ransom. Westley must rescue Buttercup to prove that true love conquers all.

This clip (over 4½ minutes)

 Start 29:47

Westley runs up the hill to meet Vizzini.

Stop 34:32   Vizzini laughs and falls over dead.

Vizzini (Wallace Shawn), the brains behind the kidnapping scheme, holds Buttercup hostage on a hilltop. Westley, having overcome both the skill of a great swordsman and the strength of a giant, finally catches up with them. Vizzini knows he can't win in a physical battle, so he accepts Westley's challenge of a battle of wits. As Vizzini's confidence turns to arrogance, he makes a fatal error in judgment, and Westley wins.

By the Book

Proverbs 16:18, 16:22

Where to take it

📺 Why was Vizzini so arrogant? Did he really believe he couldn't lose, or was he covering up his fear of losing?

📺 Was Westley just as arrogant as Vizzini or did his confidence come from something different?

📺 What's the difference between arrogance and confidence?

📺 Has pride ever put you in a humiliating situation? Explain.

📺 Is there someone in your circle of friends who always has to be right? Is it you?

📺 What would you do if someone challenged you to a battle of wits?

Trailer

Can you handle the consequences of confession?

The movie drama, PG-13

Based on actual events in the late 1950s, a lawyer working for a congressional subcommittee uncovers information that suggests certain TV quiz shows are being fixed. He focuses his investigation on the show "Twenty-One" and two of its contestants, Herbert Stempel (John Turturro) and Charles Van Doren (Ralph Fiennes). Eventually the scandal is revealed and their fraud is exposed to the nation.

This clip (6½ minutes)

Start 2:01:30

"Photographers will please clear the room."

Stop 2:07:00

"I don't think an adult of your intelligence should simply be commended for simply at long last telling the truth."

Charles Van Doren testifies before the congressional subcommittee and admits his role in the scheme to cheat on the quiz show. He takes full responsibility for his participation, knowing that while the past can't be changed, he can learn from his mistakes. Although his sorrow seems genuine, not everyone believes he should be commended for simply telling the truth. He will still be held accountable for his actions.

By the Book

Galatians 6:7; Matthew 5:13-16

Where to take it

📺 What do you think motivated Charles Van Doren to admit his mistakes? Was he truly sorry? Looking for leniency? Clearing his conscience? What motivates most people to confess?

📺 Why is it so easy to sin but so hard to confess?

📺 Should Van Doren still have been punished? Why or why not?

📺 What does it mean to be the "salt of the earth" and the "light of the world"?

📺 How do you feel after you confess a sin? Do you feel differently confessing to God than to a friend? Why?

📺 Are you in denial about something you are doing that is wrong? What can you do to come clean?

📺 How do our good deeds bring people into the kingdom? How do our bad deeds keep people away?

📺 If accepting responsibility for our wrongs doesn't pardon us from punishment, then should we do it at all? How is confession beneficial for us and the people we've hurt?

$500 What Spake Zarathul?

Trailer

Have you ever been paralyzed by your past?

The movie drama, PG-13

Rocky Balboa (Sylvester Stallone) has gained money, prestige, and popularity as a world champion boxer, but when he learns that most of his fights were staged to make him look better than he was, he questions his success. To regain his edge, he will need to defeat his past.

This clip (just under 7 minutes)

Start 1:10:28

"Look, there's just one thing you've got to remember."

Stop 1:17:20 *Rocky hugs his wife.*

In a training session on the beach, flashbacks of past fights bring back the pain and agony of the ring, and Rocky is unable to continue. He asks his wife why he was lied to and why his old coach made him think he was better than he was. For the first time in his life he admits he's afraid. Adrian (Talia Shire) tells Rocky that unless he sorts out his fears and problems, he won't be able to move on. He has to try, even if he loses.

By the Book

Philippians 3:12-14

Where to take it

- How has Rocky's past affected the way he's facing his future?

- Why is it important to forget what's behind before "straining toward what is ahead"? Is it possible to forget the past?

- Have you ever been led to believe you're good at doing something that you're really not? What did you do when you began to doubt your ability?

- What are you afraid of? Is there anything you're really afraid of losing? What can help you overcome your fear?

- Have you ever known someone who loved you enough to talk to you truthfully and lovingly? How did she impact you?

- Are you beating yourself up over your past? How can you stop?

- Read Acts 2. What part of his past was Paul trying to forget? What was the prize Paul was talking about in Philippians 3?

ROMEO AND JULIET (1996)

Trailer

Do you believe in love at first sight?

The movie drama, PG-13

In this updated version of Shakespeare's tragic play about two "star-crossed lovers," the original dialogue is retained, but the setting is changed from Verona, Italy, to modern day Verona Beach. Instead of swords, the weapons of choice are guns, and as the tragedy unfolds, Romeo and Juliet go from bliss to anguish.

This clip (under 2 minutes)

Start 31:31

Romeo, looking in a mirror, notices the aquarium.

Stop 33:26   *Romeo chases after Juliet.*

Romeo (Leonardo DiCaprio) is enchanted by fish in a colorful aquarium until he sees Juliet (Claire Danes) at an extravagant Capulet masquerade party. They are attracted to each other the first time their eyes meet. The romantic setting and music intensify their emotional reaction to each other.

By the Book

Proverbs 5:18-19; Song of Songs 4:1-7, 9-12

Where to take it

- Is love at first sight possible? What is the difference between love and infatuation?

- How much does setting (mood, music, lighting, etc.) influence the way you feel about someone?

- Describe a soul mate. Do you believe everyone has a soul mate? Explain.

- Can you really be in love with someone if you are only attracted to his appearance?

- What does it mean to really love someone?

- When someone says, "I love you," what kind of feelings do you experience?

- Do you think God has just one person on this earth for you to fall in love with? Why or why not?

Trailer

How much are you willing to sacrifice for a friend?

The movie   drama, PG

Based on the true story of Rudy Ruettiger, this film is about friendship, courage, and sacrifice. Rudy (Sean Astin) grew up in a small steel town with the dream of someday playing football for Notre Dame. Despite many obstacles, he refused to give up, and his determination inspired his friends and helped him accomplish his goal.

This clip (just over 1½ minutes)

Start 1:33:44

The interior of the coach's door.

Stop 1:35:20   *Close-up of a jersey.*

When the captain of the football team wants Rudy to take his place in the championship game, his coach tells him to do the right thing by focusing on the game, not the friendship. Believing he is doing the right thing, the captain lays down his jersey on the desk. One by one, Rudy's teammates do the same, and their coach is deeply moved by their dedication to fairness and to Rudy.

By the Book

1 John 3:16-17; John 15:13; Proverbs 17:17, 18:24

Where to take it

- What motivated the captain of the team to ask the coach to give Rudy a chance? Would you have been willing to sit out of the championship game for the sake of one player?

- Have you ever been asked to give something up for the sake of a friend? For a sister or brother? Was it easy or difficult?

- Have you ever been someone's "champion"—asking that they be given a chance to do or say something? What motivated you?

- Is it easier to sacrifice for a friend or a stranger? Why?

- What does "we ought to lay down our lives for our brothers" mean? What might you need to sacrifice to keep a friendship strong?

- What qualities do you look for in a good friend? What has Jesus' relationship with his disciples taught you about friendship?

Trailer

How eagerly do you welcome an outsider?

The movie comedy, PG

Scotty Smalls (Tom Guiry) has just moved into the
neighborhood. He wants to make friends, but every kid in
town is obsessed with baseball, and he doesn't know how to
play. Scotty is given a chance to join in a game because
Benny (Mike Vitar), the best player in town, cares enough
about fairness to stand up for him.

This clip (just under 3 minutes)

Start 19:30

"Listen. Ready? Check this out. 'I'm the great Bambino.'"

Stop 22:18   *"Man, base up, you blockheads."*

Scotty Smalls doesn't know a thing about baseball. The kids he
wants to hang out with know everything from statistics to famous
players—and their favorite player is Babe Ruth, who Scotty's never
even heard of. The kids think Scotty's a loser and try to convince
Benny to get rid of him, but Benny says Scotty stays, because—
geek or not—it's the right thing to do and it's fair.

By the Book

Acts 10:34-38; Luke 10:30-37

Where to take it

- Why is it so hard to fit in when you're the new kid in town? Have you ever had to deal with trying to make new friends and fit in?

- Why were the kids so quick to dismiss Scotty when he didn't know who Babe Ruth was? Have you made a snap judgment about someone? Were you right or wrong?

- Why do you think Benny stood up for Scotty? Would you have defended him?

- Why did Peter change his mind about preaching to the Gentiles in Acts 10?

- Why do we naturally gravitate toward people who are like us?

- Who can you be more tolerant of this week? Who can you welcome to your school, church, or neighborhood?

THE SANTA CLAUSE

Trailer

Do you need to see to believe?

The movie drama, R

After Scott Calvin (Tim Allen) accidentally knocks St. Nick off of his roof, he puts on the jolly old man's red suit and begins turning into Santa Claus. At first the changes are only physical, but as the movie progresses he becomes more like Santa Claus on the inside. Scott Calvin has a change of heart.

This clip (just over 2 minutes)

▶ Start 44:02

"I brought you some cocoa."

⬤ Stop 46:10

Scott Calvin lies down in bed next to his son.

Scott and his son have somehow been taken to the North Pole. This is quite a stretch for Scott, who doesn't believe anything he's seeing could possibly exist. Even as he's talking with an elf, he tells himself he must be dreaming. The elf explains Scott's new role as Santa Claus, part of which involves the ability to believe without seeing, the way a child would. The next thing Scott knows is, he's lying in bed next to his son, and the line between reality and fantasy blurs even more.

By the Book

John 20:29; Hebrews 11:1

Where to take it

- What did you believe as a child but no longer do? Why did you believe? Why do adults grow out of these beliefs?

- What did the elf mean when she said, "Seeing isn't believing, believing is seeing"?

- In John 20, what did Thomas need to see and do so that he could believe?

- Why does being able to see make believing easier?

- Even though we can't see God, we have seen what he's done in the world. What kind of evidence points to the existence of God?

- What is childlike faith? Can you have childlike faith and be a mature Christian? Explain.

- What changes (physical, mental, spiritual) do you see when someone is growing in their relationship with Christ?

Trailer

Why do you pray?

The movie drama, PG

This film depicts the love affair between the author C. S. "Jack" Lewis (Anthony Hopkins) and an American fan, Joy Gresham (Debra Winger). They grow to love each other after discovering they share many of the same passions and interests. Their happiness is shattered when Joy is diagnosed with terminal cancer, and the two of them must learn to make every moment together count.

This clip (just over half a minute)

"What news?"

"It doesn't change God; it changes me."

Jack's Oxford colleagues try to comfort him as he deals with the anguish of knowing that the dearest person in his life is dying of cancer. The discussion turns to the topic of prayer, and Jack clarifies his reasons for praying: he is helpless, and prayer doesn't change God—it changes him.

By the Book

James 4:1-3; Matthew 6:5-8

Where to take it

- Since God already knows our needs before we pray, why do we bother praying?

- Can prayer change God's mind?

- What are some of the physical, mental, and emotional benefits of prayer?

- Lots of people acknowledge God but not Jesus. Do you think God hears everyone's prayers or only the prayers of Christian believers?

- What are some reasons we don't get what we pray for?

- When you pray and God says no, not now, or maybe, do you get angry? What may be the reason he answers a request that way?

- What do you think Jack meant by "prayer changes me"? Do you agree with him? If so, how has prayer changed you?

- Why does God stress the reward of praying in private? What is it he wants us to develop by praying this way?

143

SHE'S HAVING A BABY

Trailer

What's it going to take for you to start counting your blessings?

The movie comedy, PG-13

Jake (Kevin Bacon) and Kristi (Elizabeth McGovern) are a young married couple in pursuit of the American dream. On the surface, Jake has it all: a beautiful house in the suburbs, a steady job at an advertising agency, a lovely wife—but it's not enough for him. In his relentless search for more and better, he finds himself tempted to look for happiness outside his marriage. It takes a life-threatening situation for Jake to discover what's really important to him and realize how much he has been taking for granted.

This clip (just over 8½ minutes)

Start 1:33:43

"Oh, hi. I was just watching...wow, here we go."

Stop 1:42:15

"And what I was looking for was not to be found but to be made."

As Jake and Kristi prepare for the birth of their first child, elation turns to fear when the doctors suddenly discover that the baby is not positioned correctly. As Jake deals with the very real possibility of losing both Kristi and the baby, he begins to see, perhaps for the first time, that everything he's ever really wanted has been right in front of him all along.

144

By the Book

Matthew 16:26; Proverbs 27:1

Where to take it

- 📺 Describe some of the memories that went through Jake's mind as he sat in the waiting room. What kind of feelings did they produce? Why do you think these memories made him reexamine his own life?

- 📺 Describe a life-changing moment or an experience that has caused you to evaluate what's really important to you.

- 📺 Have you ever felt lost? How did you find your way back?

- 📺 Give an example of something or someone you have taken for granted. What made you realize you were taking it for granted?

- 📺 Name some things for which you are grateful. Name some people. How can you show more gratefulness?

- 📺 When you think about your future, what are you concerned about? What does God say you should be concerned about?

THE SPITFIRE GRILL

Trailer

Who do you need to forgive?

The movie   drama, PG-13

When Percy (Alison Elliot) is released from prison, she retreats
to the small town of Gilead, where she finds a job and a place
to live at the Spitfire Grill. The town gives Percy a chance to
start over, and she returns the favor by bringing spirit and
enthusiasm to the lifeless community.

This clip   (over 4 minutes)

Start 1:33:28

Percy sits in a pew.

Stop 1:37:38   *"Turns out that hotel was Maine."*

Seated with a friend in an empty church, Percy confesses to
killing her stepfather. She describes the horrors of physical
and sexual abuse she endured growing up. When she was 16
and discovered that she was pregnant with her stepfather's
baby, she was frightened but vowed to protect the life
growing inside her; however, she lost the baby after being
badly beaten. Percy's regret, guilt, and victimization have not
faded, and she struggles to forgive herself, let alone believe
that God could forgive her too.

By the Book

1 John 1:8-9; Romans 8:1-2

Where to take it

- What is the significance that Percy was in church when she confessed? What was she looking for?

- Why did Percy feel guilty: because she killed her stepfather or because she didn't protect her baby?

- If you were in the church with Percy, what would you have said or done to comfort her?

- How would you explain forgiveness to someone who really needs it?

- Describe condemnation. Why are those who are in Christ free from it?

- If you know you are forgiven, why do you still have guilt and shame in your life?

- Have you ever done something you think God has never forgiven you for? What does the Bible say about God's forgiveness?

- Who do you need to forgive so that you can accept God's forgiveness?

Trailer

Are you living on God's terms or your own?

The movie   drama, PG

The film captures several years of the intertwining lives of a close-knit group of friends in a small Louisiana town. The women gather regularly at a local beauty parlor to discuss the subjects closest to their hearts: love, husbands, and family.

This clip   (just over 6 minutes)

 Start 53:32 ....

"I have no idea what to get your father."

Stop 59:48   Shelby begins to cry.

Newlywed Shelby (Julia Roberts) returns home for Christmas. She joyfully tells her mom (Sally Fields) that she is going to have a baby. Her mother's reaction is icy. Shelby asks her to be happy and begs for her support, but her mom just can't. She sees the little life growing inside her daughter as a death sentence because Shelby is diabetic and has been advised not to have children. Despite what the doctors have told her, Shelby is determined to live life on her terms, longing to experience the joy of motherhood so much that she's willing to risk her own life.

By the Book

Proverbs 15:22, 16:20, 19:20, 19:27; Ephesians 6:1-3;
    Hebrews 13:17

Where to take it

- Why didn't Shelby listen to the advice of her mother and doctors? Why don't we listen to our parents? Why don't we listen to God?

- What's the first thing you should do when you need advice? What should you consider when you're facing a difficult problem or situation?

- Why did Shelby's news upset her mother so much?

- Why does Proverbs contain so many verses on the subject of listening to instruction?

- Which advice would you have an easier time following: an adult's or a friend's? Why?

- Are people in authority or older than you always right? What implications does your answer have for taking advice from them?

- What advice did you reject that you wish you had taken? Have you ever rejected someone's advice because of who gave it (not necessarily because of what they said)? What happened?

- If you knew something could cause you pain or even death but could bring you unbelievable joy, would you do it anyway?

Trailer

Are you strong enough to walk away from a bad relationship?

The movie comedy, PG

This is the story of the Wonders, a fictional 1960s American pop rock band trying to make it big in the wake of the British Invasion. With one hit song they are propelled to the top of the charts, and their success—while brief—is memorable.

This clip (just over 2½ minutes)

Start 1:31:17

"So, it just appeared like magic?"

Stop 1:33:49   *"The same person that said you had class, Jimmy."*

Faye (Liv Tyler) is hurt by the callous attitude and put-downs of her boyfriend, Jimmy (Johnathon Schaech). Success has gone to his head and by-passed his heart. Realizing he has no long-term interest in their relationship, she tells him to stay away from her. She's ashamed of herself for denying the truth about him and wasting her emotions on him but takes full responsibility and is able to walk out of the room with her head held high, knowing she has done the right thing.

By the Book

Psalm 139:13-16; Jeremiah 1:5

Where to take it

📺 If someone's mistreating you, do you think it's possible for them to change, or should you just walk away from the relationship?

📺 What are some warning signs that a relationship is going bad?

📺 Do you think there was a reason Faye stood up for herself in front of Jimmy's friends and not when they were alone? What might her reason be?

📺 Do you think Faye made a wise decision? What finally opened her eyes? Should she have stuck it out with Jimmy?

📺 When have you walked away from something or someone you knew wasn't good for you? How did it affect your self-esteem?

📺 According to Psalm 139, who created you? What does being "fearfully and wonderfully made" mean to you?

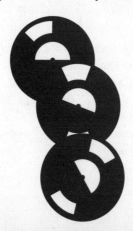

Trailer

When you look at someone, do you see color or character?

The movie drama, R

A young black girl was raped and brutally beaten by two white men. Afraid that they would get away with the murder the way men in a neighboring county did, the girl's father, Carl Lee Hailey (Samuel L. Jackson) shot them in a southern Mississippi courtroom in front of numerous witnesses. Now his fate is in the hands of a young white lawyer, Jake Brigance (Matthew McConaughey), who risks his own life to defend the grieving father.

This clip (under 8 minutes)

Start 2:16:55

Jake gets up from the defense table.

Stop 2:24:35 *"The defense rests your honor."*

Jake addresses the jury, seeking honesty and truth. He tells them that until people can see each other as equals, justice will never be realized, and he doesn't honestly feel a black man can get a fair trial in the South. Jake depicts the brutality of the little girl's rape in graphic detail, asking the jury to imagine her victimization, and ending with an unexpected twist that sets up the entire defense.

By the Book

Romans 2:11; Deuteronomy 10:17

Where to take it

- 📺 Do you think Carl Lee's actions were justified? Why or why not? Would your parents have done the same? Would they have thought about it? If you were the child's parent, what would you have done?

- 📺 How did you feel while you were watching this scene?

- 📺 How far would you go if a loved one was hurt? Would you take justice into your own hands?

- 📺 What does it mean that "God does not show favoritism"? What does God see when he looks at you?

- 📺 Do you agree or disagree with this statement: Everyone has some degree of racial prejudice.

- 📺 Have you ever felt ashamed of yourself for being prejudiced in some way, whether you acted upon it or just thought it? What are some prejudices you have (not just racial). Be honest!

- 📺 If Dr. Martin Luther King, Jr., were alive today, would he be proud of or disappointed in our efforts toward racial equality? How powerful a force is racism today?

- 📺 Have you ever felt like a victim of prejudice because you are Christian?

- 📺 How can you conquer your prejudices? How can you help victims of prejudice or people who are prejudiced?

Trailer

Will you ever give up on the lost?

The movie drama, PG-13

This is the story of two fictional lovers on the tragic maiden voyage of R.M.S. Titanic. Bound for America in 1912, the "unsinkable" luxury liner strikes an iceberg on a frozen arctic night, and over 1,500 people perish in the icy water.

This clip (just under 1½ minutes)

Start tape 2, 1:04:26

The boat approaches the dead bodies.

Stop 1:05:54   *"Can anyone hear me?"*

After the great ship sinks, only a portion of its passengers survive in lifeboats. One crew member decides he can't give up hope and goes on a desperate search, looking for the slightest sign of life in the cold, icy waters. As the lifeboat floats through a sea of dead bodies, the surviving passengers are overcome by agony and despair.

By the Book

2 Corinthians 6:2; Acts 1:8; Luke 15:3-10

Where to take it

- How does this scene from Titanic relate to lost souls on earth?

- What is heaven like? Hell?

- In the stories Jesus told in Luke 15, what happened when something of value was lost? What happened when the lost were found?

- What point was Jesus trying to make in the parables in Luke 15?

- Will it ever be too late for people to receive the gift of salvation? What support do you have for your answer?

Trailer

Are you letting your temper get the best of you?

The movie comedy, PG-13

Tommy Callahan, Jr. (Chris Farley), a bumbling, fairly dim-witted college graduate, is suddenly responsible for running his family's auto parts business after his father dies of a heart attack. The only hope for the company (and the factory town built around it) is for Tommy to sell a new line of brake pads to nationwide auto part stores. He and Richard (David Spade), the uptight assistant of the late Tommy, Sr., hit the road to save the factory.

This clip (under 3 minutes)

Start 59:45

The car hood flies up in Tommy's face.

Stop 1:02:03   *"Hey, prehistoric forest!"*

The road has not been kind to these two unfortunate salesmen, and Richard's patience is wearing thin. The hood of Richard's car flies up, resulting in a frightening ride down the freeway, and Richard tries to blame Tommy. Richard takes a cheap shot at Tommy's dad, starting a heated argument, which escalates into a fist fight. Later, they face each other at dinner, embarrassed and ashamed, unwilling to be honest about what happened between them, and unable to heal.

156

By the Book

Ephesians 4:26-27

Where to take it

   What caused this fight between Tommy and Richard? How could it have been avoided?

   What does "in your anger do not sin" mean?

   How does anger give the devil a foothold? Have you ever gone to bed angry at someone? What do these verses say the danger in doing so is?

   What are some common reasons friendships end?

   Do you hold grudges for a long time? If so, how does Ephesians 4 affect you?

   When was the last time you had a fight with your best friend? What did you fight about? Did either or both of you apologize? Did you talk to each other about what happened?

   If you had been Tommy or Richard, would you have handled the fallout from the fight differently?

TOY STORY

Trailer

Are you so busy comparing yourself to others that you've forgotten who you are?

The movie family, G

A little boy named Andy has a room full of toys that come to life when he isn't there. Life is pleasant except for the fear that comes with birthdays and Christmas, because those are the times when new toys arrive. That's when they could be...replaced! But Woody the Cowboy isn't afraid. He's supremely confident of his status as Andy's favorite toy—that is, until Buzz Lightyear comes along.

This clip (just under 6 minutes)

Start 25:05

"What is it?"

Stop 31:02 *"They'll see. I'm still Andy's favorite toy."*

Andy's mom pulls out a surprise birthday present that becomes the hit of the party. It's Buzz Lightyear, Space Ranger—the hottest, newest, gadget-loaded toy around! The kids rush upstairs to play with him and in the frenzy of activity, Woody is knocked off the bed. Buzz makes quite an impression on all of Andy's toys with his recorded voice, laser beam, and stories of defending the galaxy—all that is, except Woody, who is clearly irritated at the attention this brash new intruder is receiving.

By the Book

James 3:13-18; Exodus 20:17

Where to take it

📺 Do you think Woody was more concerned about how Andy felt about him or what the toys were thinking about him?

📺 What are some of the emotions you feel when a close friend becomes friends with someone else?

📺 How is Woody's experience similar to what you experience when a boyfriend or girlfriend rejects you?

📺 What do you think causes people to compare (themselves, their children, their parents, their possessions) to others?

📺 Are you envious of your friends because of things they have? If you had those things, do you think your life would be better? How?

📺 What do you think it would take for you to be more self-confident? How do you think feeling more self-confident would affect the way people think about you?

📺 Why do you think first impressions can be deceiving?

Trailer

What if the whole world was watching you?

The movie — drama, PG-13

Truman Burbank (Jim Carrey) couldn't have suspected that the beautiful seaside town where he grew up was just a gigantic stage, and that his life was actually one of the most popular shows on TV. Adopted as a baby by the show's producer-director, Truman's entire life has been a secret broadcast, with friends and family members the actors, and Truman himself in the lead role. Everyone knows Truman, but Truman doesn't know it.

This clip (5 minutes)

Start 37:00

"And it's another beautiful day in paradise."

Stop 42:00 — *Truman runs into the market.*

As Truman drives to work, the music on the radio is interrupted by what seems to be actors getting directions from a control booth. What they say eerily parallels the activity around him, and although they hastily recover and the music resumes, Truman is suspicious. Paranoia turns to panic as he realizes he's being watched.

By the Book

1 Peter 2:12; Titus 2:6-8

Where to take it

📺 What would you do differently if you knew there was a camera on you all day, every day?

📺 Is the way you behave at home the same or different from the way you behave in public? How?

📺 Have you ever felt like you were always being watched? Without giving names, who did you feel was watching, and how did it make you feel?

📺 If you could watch someone's life, who would you choose? (Pick one person you know and one person from the Bible.)

📺 Describe a time when things weren't quite what they seemed to be.

📺 Have you ever met a celebrity? How were they the same or different from their TV or movie image? How?

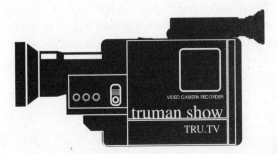

Trailer

Do you know what you're looking for?

The movie music/documentary, PG-13

This documentary chronicles the Irish rock group's 1987-88 tour of North America. The band travels to different venues and performs many of their most popular songs.

This clip (just over 4½ minutes)

Start 15:09

"Well, we wrote the song, 'I Still Haven't Found What I'm Looking For.'"

Stop 19:46 The song ends.

The band goes to a church in Harlem and sings "I Still Haven't Found What I'm Looking For" with a gospel choir. The song's theme resembles the message of Ecclesiastes: searching to fill the emptiness in our lives with adventure, relationships, and riches. The choir brings astonishing depth and intensity to an already powerful secular song.

By the Book

John 4:13-14; Ecclesiastes 1:2, 2:24-26; Matthew 16:26

Where to take it

- What is the songwriter looking for?

- Where did he look? Why didn't he find it?

- Before she met Jesus, what was the Samaritan woman at the well (John 4) looking for? Where did she look? How did her encounter with Jesus change her? Did she find what she was looking for?

- What type of things did Solomon deem "meaningless" in the first two chapters of Ecclesiastes? Can you relate?

- Why do things that are supposed to bring us satisfaction still leaves us feeling empty? Name something you thought would be fulfilling but left you empty.

- How does Jesus' living water quench our thirsts?

- What are some similarities between what the world is looking for and what Christians are looking for? Dissimilarities?

Trailer

What if everyone got what they deserved?

The movie drama, PG-13

Stu Simmons (Elijah Wood) and his sister are fighting a war they never wanted, but they find themselves cornered, with battle their only option. Several bullies in their Mississippi town have singled out Stu as their next target. Stu seeks backup and support from his Vietnam veteran father (Kevin Costner), but his dad's tactics of peace and tolerance make little sense to him.

This clip (just over 2½ minutes)

Start 1:02:40

"Dad! Dad!"

Stop 1:05:13

"They look like they haven't been given anything in a long time."

At a country fair, the bullies antagonize Stu, who's finally had enough and fights back. Stu's father steps in and breaks it up. After the crowd of onlookers has moved on, he gives cotton candy to the bullies. Confused and angry, Stu asks his dad how he could be so kind to the kids who just beat him up. His father replies, "They look like they haven't been given anything in a long time."

By the Book

Matthew 5:38-42, 20:16

Where to take it

- Do you feel like God owes you because you do good things? What does Matthew 20 teach us about this attitude?

- Why were his father's actions so shocking to Stu? How would you have reacted if you were Stu? Are you more like Stu or his father?

- What did the bullies' reaction tell you they felt when they were offered the cotton candy? Describe a time you've felt that way.

- How are Stu's father's actions similar to Jesus' commands in Matthew 5? How are they similar to the landowner's actions in the parable of the workers in the vineyard (Matthew 20)?

- Have you ever been the victim of a bully? How did you handle him?

- Do you think treating a bully with kindness would work? Why or why not?

- Have you ever given someone something they didn't deserve? What was their reaction? How did you feel?

- How can grace and mercy help us win our battles?

- How can you show mercy? Who are some people that need to see you demonstrate grace?

WAYNE'S WORLD

Trailer

Do you have what it takes to be a best friend?

The movie   comedy, PG-13

Wayne (Mike Myers) and Garth (Dana Carvey) are two guys from suburban Chicago with their own local-access cable TV show. The show is a huge hit, and after a producer and sponsors enter the picture, Wayne and Garth begin to make a lot of money from something that started out as a hobby. The pressures of stardom strain their relationship, but they learn to resolve their differences.

This clip (just over 1½ minutes)

Start 33:33

Wayne and Garth are sitting on the hood of the Pinto and Garth is whistling.

Stop 35:18   An airplane flies overhead.

Best friends Wayne and Garth share a special moment, looking up at the stars and talking about life and love. It's nothing out of the ordinary; they're just doing what good friends do best.

By the Book

Proverbs 17:17, 18:24, 27:17; Ecclesiastes 4:7-12

Where to take it

📺 What things did Wayne and Garth discuss that they wouldn't share with anyone else?

📺 According to the verses, what are some of the benefits of close friendships? What are some qualities a good friend has?

📺 How has a friendship helped you through adversity?

📺 What are some things that can turn a casual relationship into a friendship?

📺 Who is your best friend? What makes her your best friend? How has this friendship influenced you?

📺 What qualities do you have that make you a good friend to have?

📺 If someone asked your friends to describe you, what do you think they would say?

📺 What are some similarities between the way you love a brother or sister and the way you love a friend? Differences?

📺 What are some things you've discovered about Jesus that make him the best friend you could ever have?

Trailer

Is personal pain destroying you?

The movie comedy, PG-13

Robbie Hart (Adam Sandler) used to be the lead singer of a rock band, but his band wasn't as successful as he dreamed and now they only play wedding receptions and bar mitzvahs. When his fiancée leaves him at the altar, Robbie is heartbroken and turns to Julia (Drew Barrymore) for comfort. Julia is engaged, but before long realizes she may be about to marry the wrong man.

This clip (under 2½ minutes)

Start 41:35

"You know, it's funny some of us will never find true love."

Stop 44:03   *"Love stinks."*

Robbie is still reeling from his break-up, but the show must go on. He has a wedding reception to do. He shows up in wrinkled, dirty clothes, and his anger and tension are quite obvious. After numerous digs at his audience, the joy of the newly married couple gets to him, and he sings "Love Stinks"—the very antithesis of a love song—ruining the wedding reception.

By the Book

Psalm 34:18, 147:3

Where to take it

📺 Can you relate to Robbie's situation? When you have broken up with someone, how does it make you feel to see two people in love?

📺 Describe a time you've broken up with someone and someone has broken up with you. What were some of the emotions you felt?

📺 What kind of lessons have you learned from breakups?

📺 What are some healthy and unhealthy ways to deal with disappointment?

📺 Why do many people feel they have to be dating to be happy?

📺 Describe a time when you felt God was close to you in the midst of pain.

WHEN A MAN LOVES A WOMAN

Trailer

Have you ever had to admit to an addiction?

The movie drama, R

The joys Alice (Meg Ryan) shared with her two kids and passionate husband decreased as her dependence on alcohol increased. Now she has to admit her addiction, stay sober, and seek accountability and forgiveness, so that she can regain her joy and find peace.

This clip (over 4 minutes)

Start 1:58:11

"Hi, I'm Alice."

Stop 2:02:28 *Alice holds up her gold chip and the audience applauds.*

Alice gives her testimony at a 12-step meeting for addicts. She's taken a big step by admitting her craving for alcohol. Miserable that her children and husband have been victims of her alcoholic rages, she seeks their forgiveness as she seeks to forgive herself.

By the Book

Proverbs 23:29-35; James 5:16

Where to take it

- Name some things people are easily addicted to.

- Is alcoholism a disease? Why or why not?

- Would you say alcohol is a drug? Why or why not?

- According to Proverbs 23, what are some of the consequences of alcohol abuse?

- Why did it take Alice so long to accept the truth about her problem? Why do so many alcoholics have trouble admitting their addiction?

- What are some reasons people abuse alcohol, drugs, and other substances?

- How does an alcoholic kick his habit?

- Do you think any addict can ever completely recover? Why or why not?

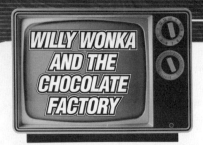

Trailer

Is greed getting in the way of what you need?

The movie **family, G**

Five children have won the much coveted prize of a personally guided tour of the Willy Wonka Chocolate Factory. Before they can enter the factory, however, they must sign a contract agreeing not to eat anything, which will be next to impossible since they will be surrounded by candy everywhere they look. One by one, each child succumbs to the temptations of the factory.

This clip **(just under 3 minutes)**

Start 1:10:02

"This stuff is terrific."

Stop 1:12:54   "Like the Oompah-Lumpah doopidie do. Doopidie do."

Augustus (Michael Bollner) is the first to give in to his temptation. As he kneels down to drink from the milk chocolate river that flows through the factory, he falls in and is pulled under. Willy Wonka (Gene Wilder) seems more concerned about the river becoming contaminated than about Augustus' safety. Being a large boy, Augustus gets stuck in a pipe, but enough pressure builds to send him rocketing into the fudge room.

By the Book

1 Timothy 6:6-8; Luke 12:15, 22:1-6

Where to take it

- Is there anything you are continually tempted by, no matter what you do? What is it? Why does it tempt you?

- Do you see any similarities between Willy Wonka and Satan—the way they work, how they tempt, their attitudes?

- What are some of the consequences of greed and gluttony?

- Why are so many people discontented with what they have? Describe someone you know (without giving names) who seems discontent and why you think they feel that way. What do you think would make her happier?

- Too much of a good thing can be bad. Give some examples.

- Was money the only factor that motivated Judas' decision to betray Jesus? What else could have influenced him?

- What are some places or things you need to avoid when you start feeling restless and discontent?

- How can you raise your levels of contentment and moderation?

RESOURCES FROM YOUTH SPECIALTIES

Professional Resources
Administration, Publicity, & Fundraising (Ideas Library)
Developing Student Leaders
Equipped to Serve: Volunteer Youth Worker Training Course
Help! I'm a Junior High Youth Worker!
Help! I'm a Small-Group Leader!
Help! I'm a Sunday School Teacher!
Help! I'm a Volunteer Youth Worker!
How to Expand Your Youth Ministry
How to Speak to Youth...and Keep Them Awake at the Same Time
Junior High Ministry (Updated & Expanded)
The Ministry of Nurture: A Youth Worker's Guide to Discipling Teenagers
One Kid at a Time: Reaching Youth through Mentoring
Purpose-Driven Youth Ministry
So That's Why I Keep Doing This! 52 Devotional Stories for Youth Workers
A Youth Ministry Crash Course
The Youth Worker's Handbook to Family Ministry

Youth Ministry Programming
Camps, Retreats, Missions, & Service Ideas (Ideas Library)
Compassionate Kids: Practical Ways to Involve Your Students in Mission and Service
Creative Bible Lessons from the Old Testament
Creative Bible Lessons in 1 & 2 Corinthians
Creative Bible Lessons in John: Encounters with Jesus
Creative Bible Lessons in Romans: Faith on Fire!
Creative Bible Lessons on the Life of Christ
Creative Junior High Programs from A to Z, Vol. 1 (A-M)
Creative Junior High Programs from A to Z, Vol. 2 (N-Z)
Creative Meetings, Bible Lessons, & Worship Ideas (Ideas Library)
Crowd Breakers & Mixers (Ideas Library)
Drama, Skits, & Sketches (Ideas Library)
Drama, Skits, & Sketches 2 (Ideas Library)
Dramatic Pauses
Everyday Object Lessons
Games (Ideas Library)
Games 2 (Ideas Library)
Great Fundraising Ideas for Youth Groups
More Great Fundraising Ideas for Youth Groups
Great Retreats for Youth Groups
Greatest Skits on Earth
Greatest Skits on Earth, Vol. 2
Holiday Ideas (Ideas Library)
Hot Illustrations for Youth Talks
More Hot Illustrations for Youth Talks
Still More Hot Illustrations for Youth Talks
Incredible Questionnaires for Youth Ministry

Junior High Game Nights
More Junior High Game Nights
Kickstarters: 101 Ingenious Intros to Just about Any Bible Lesson
Live the Life! Student Evangelism Training Kit
Memory Makers
Play It! Great Games for Groups
Play It Again! More Great Games for Groups
Special Events (Ideas Library)
Spontaneous Melodramas
Super Sketches for Youth Ministry
Teaching the Bible Creatively
Videos That Teach
What Would Jesus Do? Youth Leader's Kit
WWJD—The Next Level
Wild Truth Bible Lessons
Wild Truth Bible Lessons 2
Wild Truth Bible Lessons—Pictures of God
Worship Services for Youth Groups

Discussion Starters

Discussion & Lesson Starters (Ideas Library)
Discussion & Lesson Starters 2 (Ideas Library)
Get 'Em Talking
Keep 'Em Talking!
High School TalkSheets
More High School TalkSheets
High School TalkSheets: Psalms and Proverbs
Junior High TalkSheets
More Junior High TalkSheets
Junior High TalkSheets: Psalms and Proverbs
What If...? 450 Thought-Provoking Questions to Get Teenagers Talking,
    Laughing, and Thinking
Would You Rather...? 465 Provocative Questions to Get Teenagers Talking
Have You Ever...? 450 Intriguing Questions Guaranteed to Get Teenagers Talking

Clip Art

ArtSource: Stark Raving Clip Art (print)
ArtSource: Youth Group Activities (print)
ArtSource CD-ROM: Clip Art Library Version 2.0

Videos

EdgeTV
The Heart of Youth Ministry: A Morning with Mike Yaconelli
Next Time I Fall in Love Video Curriculum
Understanding Your Teenager Video Curriculum

Student Books

Grow For It Journal
Grow For It Journal through the Scriptures
Teen Devotional Bible
What Would Jesus Do? Spiritual Challenge Journal
WWJD Spiritual Challenge Journal: The Next Level
Wild Truth Journal for Junior Highers
Wild Truth Journal—Pictures of God